John Dickinson

Dhar not restored

In Spite of the House of Commons and of public Opinion

John Dickinson

Dhar not restored

In Spite of the House of Commons and of public Opinion

ISBN/EAN: 9783337151584

Printed in Europe, USA, Canada, Australia, Japan

Cover: Foto ©ninafisch / pixelio.de

More available books at **www.hansebooks.com**

DHAR NOT RESTORED;

IN SPITE OF

THE HOUSE OF COMMONS,

AND OF

PUBLIC OPINION.

BY

JOHN DICKINSON, F.R.A.S., &c., &c.

"I wish deliberately to record my fixed opinion that our immediate possessions are at present very much too large,—too large for us to defend; too large for us to administer; too large for us to instruct."

"The Empire in India," by Major Evans Bell, page 399.

London:
P. S. KING, 34, PARLIAMENT STREET, S.W.

1864.

[PRICE ONE SHILLING.]

To LORDS ELLENBOROUGH & STANLEY,

THE FIRST MINISTERS FOR INDIA,

WHO AFTER A LONG INTERVAL

REVIVED, BY WORD AND DEED,

THE HOPES OF INDIAN PRINCES AND PEOPLE

IN THE JUSTICE OF THE BRITISH GOVERNMENT,—

THESE PAGES ARE RESPECTFULLY DEDICATED.

PREFACE.

THE bearings of the Dhar case may not at first sight be apparent in England; the vexed question of right in so small a territory, may not appear to deserve the careful and elaborate argument which I now publish.

In India, on the contrary, it is felt that this case is of such paramount importance, as a precedent, that it not only must affect the decision of a number of other cases now pending, but involves ultimately the destiny of every surviving Native State.

For if, after all the stir that has been made about this case, the India authorities are able at last to carry their point, and retain their grasp of Dhar, by a combination of active and passive resistance, of evasion, deception, and procrastination, that in the end has *tired out* the public, it will be hopeless to fight any future battle to save a Native State, and the precedent of Dhar (followed immediately by those of Mysore and Oodeypore), will become as decisive of a new system of annexation, as the precedent of Sattara was of the old one.

The process is, in Hamlet's phrase, "as easy as " lying,"—'tis but a certain amount of British " manage- " ment," and lo! the population are " considered as " British subjects,"* and the prince is considered to have "a fair allowance " out of his own revenues!

> " . . . . Last scene of all,
> " That ends this strange, eventful history :"

A cabinet minister says, as one has said to me before now, " Pensioned princes, clinging to an useless and " absurd State, and prevented by this from becoming " in any way useful members of society, are a class " whose extinction I should be glad to see." And so their knell is knolled!

But is the annexation question to be settled thus easily? Can we so soon again listen to the flippant, shallow, immoral reasonings which, only seven years ago, caused the fearful deaths of men, women, and

---

* " The Province of Mysore is not to be handed over for direct " administration of its Government to His Highness the Maharajah : " the country is to be considered as British soil, and its population of " four millions as British subjects; and the arrival of the formal " despatch upon the subject from the Council of India is all that is " waited for to unite Coorg with it, under the name of the Mysore " Provinces. Shall we now have the new offices in Bangalore ?— *Bangalore Herald.* "Allen's Indian Mail," February 12th, 1864.

children, by tens of thousands, and the waste of forty millions sterling within a few months, besides sowing broadcast those seeds of hatred which may be still growing on to some appointed hour of judgment and retribution? I say "still growing," for we learn nothing of the heart of India from loyal addresses drawn up by the wealthy, pacific, enlightened* inhabitants of the Presidency towns, and "prosperity" letters read out to the House of Commons; we had plenty of such things before the Rebellion, plenty of such addresses even during the Rebellion, when deeds within the Mofussil formed a horrible contrast to words from without.

What, then, is the fatal illusion that tempts our government to begin once more the "grasping" system in India? It is the illusion of irresistible force. It is the presence of 80,000 British soldiers in that empire! If, they think, less than half that number, barely 35,000 Englishmen, sufficed to break the neck of a rebellion supported by a regular army of 70,000 Natives, the whole number, 80,000 British soldiers, with no such army to fear, and the people disarmed, enable them to do what they like with the country!

---

* Though they prove that "Education" is one of our best allies in India.

This it is which hardens and blinds our statesmen, and makes them, like Macbeth,—

> ". . . . take no care
> "Who chafes, who frets, or where conspirers are."

This it is which suggests to old partisans of "the "Company" the frequent taunt: "We told you India "Reformers how it would be; you have realised "all the mischief of Fox's India bill; you have "given the government such an amount of Indian "patronage, that a ministry once planted is virtually "irremovable by the House of Commons." As if India Reformers were responsible for arrangements against which they uniformly protested! As if they would have voted for an army of 80,000 British soldiers in India, when it was plainly announced from the first, as one of the greatest recommendations of the plan, that by the help of the railways it would always enable the government "*to detach from India to Europe a seasoned,* "*practical, and efficient army of from* 30,000 *to* 40,000 "*men.*"*. One of the wisest and best of India Reformers at once warned the country that, if so, there was no security for our liberties at home; if, on any occasion of popular excitement, the government could

---

* "India; its Government, Misgovernment, and Future, considered." By R. J. R. Campbell, M.P., a resident of twenty-five years' experience in India.

in a few weeks pour in such an army from India, used to flesh their swords on semi-civilised races till they acquired an utter indifference to human life, like those Algerine soldiers òf France who were so ready to sweep the streets of Paris with their fusillades.*

Then, it may be said, do I deny the existence of danger in India? I do deny the existence of any danger *from within*, that we do not wantonly and knowingly, from corrupt motives, create for ourselves, either by maintaining an excessive military force, or by a system of confiscation which drives those Native Princes and landowners to despair, who, until their possessions are threatened, are bound by their strongest interests to support us. I do not deny the existence of danger *from without*. On the contrary, ever since I

---

* " Are we," said he, " resolutely to shut our eyes to the lessons of " history on this subject? How were the liberties of Rome destroyed? " Precisely in this way. The extent of her conquests compelled her " to maintain immense armies in her remote provinces; and these, " when summoned back, became the willing instruments of tyranny at " home. ' The decline of Rome,' says Gibbon, ' was the natural and " ' inevitable effect of immoderate greatness. Prosperity ripened the " ' principle of decay; the causes of destruction multiplied with the " ' extent of conquest; and, as soon as time or accident had removed " ' the artificial supports, the stupendous fabric yielded to the pressure " ' of its own weight. The story of its ruin is simple and obvious; " ' and, instead of enquiring *why* the Roman Empire was destroyed, we " ' should rather be surprised that it had subsisted so long. *The* " ' *victorious legions, who in distant wars acquired the vices of strangers* " ' *and mercenaries, first oppressed the freedom of the republic, and* " ' *afterwards violated the majesty of the purple.*' "—" The Present and " Future of India," by Henry Richard.

read the volume as a boy, I have never been able to shake off the foreboding expressed by Nicholls, in his "Recollections," that the downfall of the British empire would begin by a struggle with 'a combination of civilised rivals for the possession of India (like that "League of Cambrai" which began the ruin of Venice). Such a combination has often been projected. I have reason to believe that it is steadily kept in view; and, if ever it comes, it will show at once that we have been mad in relying on mere brute force to hold India against the will of the people, though we shall be so mad if our punishment is decreed. It is a proverb, that "Quem Deus vult perdere prius dementat."

If ever that danger from without arrives, the illusion of our irresistible force will be dispelled at once. Independently of our difficulty in recruiting, owing to the emigration, which is now extending from Ireland to England, the public will of course require half of our 80,000 British soldiers at home; and the remainder, in India, when attacked from without, will be paralysed by the hostility of the people, and unable to preserve their communications; and then will begin the downfall of the British empire. On the other hand, if we chose to make the people of India friends instead of enemies, I am sure we might hold that empire with an army of 40,000 Englishmen, against all the civilised nations who would ever unite against us. But I admit that it will be no easy matter now to regain the goodwill and confidence of the natives. To do it we must entirely reverse our past, and much of our present, policy; in one word, *we must keep the promises made to the people of India in the Queen's Proclamation!*

But it is said by some crafty defenders of the old policy, that our constant territorial extension in India (which, be it remembered, has absorbed thousands of private landed estates, as well as a score of kingdoms), has been, not voluntary on our parts, but a necessity,* forced upon us by Providence; that it was a divine dispensation, to spread true religion and civilisation, and, in their phrase, "to win India to Christ." Now I flatly deny this doctrine of necessity. I do not believe, although it may please God to bring good out of evil, that he ever forces us to commit crimes, which are forbidden by his law, and threatened with his vengeance. It is not God, but the Devil, that "enters into the "heart" of those who betray their friends; and it is the peculiar scandal of our system, in Native opinion, that we are always grasping the possessions of our "friends." And I have another special reason for

---

* " So spake the fiend; and with necessity,
" The tyrant's plea, excused his devilish acts."
Paradise Lost.

denying the necessity of our territorial extension in India, which is this—that I have examined all the public, and many of the private, acts of spoliation which we have committed in that empire for years past, and I never found one which was necessary. I have now shown in detail that it was not necessary in the case of Dhar, because, besides being an illustration of the past, this case will be a precedent for the future, at a time when the "grasping" system is beginning again in India; and the public must decide whether it is to be sanctioned by this country or not.

CONTENTS.

―――o―――

Chapter I.
Introduction—Reasons for publishing this Work 1

Chapter II.
Action in England on learning the confiscation of Dhar—Orders of the Home Government under Lord Stanley to restore the Principality eventually to the young Rajah 4

Chapter III.
General circumstances which rendered every State in Central India unable to control its mercenary troops during the summer of 1857 10

Chapter IV.
Two special circumstances which made the State of Dhar more unable than other States to control its mercenary troops 24

Chapter V.
Action in India on receiving Lord Stanley's orders to restore the Principality eventually to its young Rajah—Decision not to restore it 51

Chapter VI.
Notices of the subject in the House of Commons—Second promise of the Home Government under Sir Charles Wood to restore Dhar to its Rajah, and evasion of this promise............. 82

Chapter VII.
Conclusion—Two distinct policies are in presence on this occasion— Old political parties are resisting a new policy 90

Appendices 97

DHAR NOT RESTORED.

CHAPTER I.

INTRODUCTION—*Reasons for publishing this Work.*

It is generally believed by the public, and has been asserted by recent Anglo-Indian writers of authority,* that a conspicuous example of renouncing the "annexa-" tion policy" which preceded the rebellion, was afforded by the restoration of Dhar to its Native prince. This general belief is founded on the following most explicit and unequivocal promise of Sir Charles Wood to the House of Commons, in answer to a question by Lord Stanley, on March 13th, 1860.

"Sir Charles Wood said, the noble Lord was quite "right in stating that during the period of his con-" tinuance in office no answer had been received to the "communication to which he referred. Late in the "autumn, however, a dispatch had reached the India "Office from Lord Canning, in which he justified the "course he had pursued in reference to the annexation, "and pointed out the future steps which he recom-

---

* Mr. Montgomery Martin, Major Evans Bell, &c.

" mended to be taken. Having considered the subject
" fully, Her Majesty's Government had determined to
" adhere in the main to the advice which was con-
" tained in the dispatch which the noble Lord (Lord
" Stanley) had addressed to the Government of India,
" and Lord Canning had accordingly been directed to
" retain possession of the State of Dhar only until the
" heir to it should come of age, when he was to be
" restored to the territory which belonged to him. The
" only exception which had been made in the case was
" that of the outlying district which we had adminis-
" tered for many years, and which had paid to the
" Native Ruler a much larger sum than that which we
" had received from it. It had been deemed to be
" only right that when we were taxing our own loyal
" subjects in India for the expenses of the war, some
" contribution should be made by those whose mis-
" conduct had entailed that expense. Her Majesty's
" Government had therefore directed that the payment
" on account of the outlying district to which he
" referred should no longer be made to the Chief of
" Dhar, by which the revenues of India would be saved
" from a charge of between £2,000 and £3,000 per
" annum."*

This ministerial promise was not the only reason I had for sharing in the general belief that Dhar was restored to its Rajah. I thought it so much a point of honour with several important Members of Parliament to insist on justice being done in this case, that the Indian Minister would not venture to break the engagement he had thus publicly made with the House of Commons and the country, and therefore I gave no

* Hansard's Debates, 2nd vol. of Session 1860, page 446.

heed to rumours which reached me from time to time of a breach of faith in India.

However, last autumn, to my extreme surprise and mortification, I received certain information that the Government of Dhar was not restored to the young prince, and that there was evidently no intention of restoring it. Under these circumstances I have felt it my duty to bring the whole case* once more before the public, and to enter more into detail than I should have done if this story was fresh in men's minds, because few gentlemen may now retain a vivid recollection of events which happened five or six years ago.

* As I may have occasion to refer to several facts and documents not yet in the possession of the public, I may as well observe that these facts and documents are all on record in the archives of Dhar, and have been carefully verified by English eyes before I used them, so that such new evidence will be forthcoming if required.

CHAPTER II.

Action in England on learning the Confiscation of Dhar— Orders of the Home Government under Lord Stanley to restore the Principality eventually to the young Rajah.

ON Sunday, the 21st of March, 1858, I received from India the distressing news that the Government had confiscated the State of Dhar. On Monday, the 22nd, I wrote to the President of the Board of Control (then Lord Ellenborough), stating that not only was there no justification whatever for this particular act of spoliation, but that the immediate revival of a system of spoliation was a shocking return for that personal assistance of the Native princes, which had been so thankfully acknowledged by our countrymen the year before, and had contributed so greatly to save our empire; and that such an act was in flat contradiction with those principles of public policy which Lord Ellenborough had himself proclaimed with such energy in his evidence before the Select Committee of 1852,* and which I quoted in my letter.

On Tuesday, March 23rd, I asked Mr. J. B. Smith to put a question in the House of Commons about the confiscation of Dhar, to which the Indian Secretary, Mr. Baillie, replied that Her Majesty's Government had

* *Vide* Appendix·A.

no information from India on the subject. I learnt, from continual enquiries at the India Office, that Her Majesty's Government remained without such information until the month of May; but, on the 11th of June, in answer to another question by Mr. J. B. Smith, the Minister for India, then Lord Stanley, informed the public that it was the intention of the Home Government " to disallow the policy of annexation as " regards the territory of Dhar, and that the present " occupation of that territory was provisional only."*

In the despatch conveying that decision to India, June 22nd, 1858, the Home Government, after recapitulating the facts, thus explained the reasons for their decision. "The ground upon which this forfeiture was " declared, and, as we learn from subsequent papers, has " since been carried into effect, was, that it is expedient " to demonstrate in the most unmistakable manner, to " the princes and chiefs of Malwa, that the British " Government holds the Durbars responsible for the " conduct of their armies, and has determined there-" fore, in this case, by way of example, to visit upon " the state itself the rebellion of its mercenary troops. " But we do not perceive how we could consistently " punish this or any other weak state for its inability to " control its troops, when it was patent to the whole " world that the more powerful states of Gwalior and " Indore, and even the British Government itself, were " unable to control theirs."†

The Home Government therefore directed that the

---

* Hansard, 2nd vol. of Session 1857-58, page 574.

† Parliamentary Paper, No 200 of 1859, page 5.

attachment of the State should only continue during the investigations of the Indian Government as to the instigators of the outrages committed by the mercenary troops; that the members of the Dhar Durbar already arrested on that charge, and sent prisoners to Mhow, should be punished if convicted; but arrangements should be made for eventually restoring his " inherit-" ance" to the young Rajah, "in consideration of his " youth and apparent innocence, and the good conduct " of his predecessor in this ancient principality."

They concluded by desiring the Indian Government, in case any circumstances with which they were not yet acquainted should justify the alienation of the State from the Puar family, to consider and report to them for their instructions, in what manner it might be appropriated as a reward to one of our native allies.

Such was the tenor of this excellent despatch, in which there was only one passage that I seriously object to, namely, that which affirms, para. 3, that the Indian Governments having "suffered" the adoption of Balla Sahib to take effect, "was a mark of especial " favour."

The analysis of this single phrase will give a deep insight into the sort of India government which preceded the rebellion. Here is a case in which the Government had no sort of claim, private or public, to the estate of its deceased *friend*,—a case in which it did not even question the right of its late friend's (legal as well as adopted) heir to his "inheritance," and yet the Government considers it, not an act of simple justice, but " of especial favor," to allow the " heir " to take *what was his own by law!* It may be said: Surely, when

Lord Dalhousie's Government had been robbing crowds of heirs,* whose claims by law as well as adoption were as good as those of Balla Sahib, it was an act of "favor" not to rob him too. Perhaps so; but it is difficult to imagine a community where it was so habitual for the strong friend to rob his weaker ones, that when somebody was not robbed, he was told to consider it "*a mark of especial favor!*" It is something revolting to the Western world to imagine such a state of things, and when the India Government thus openly and contemptuously set aside those notions of law and order, and respect for the rights of property, which become an instinct in civilized minds, and which are the best, the only secure and durable foundation of political power; when it did this by an eight years' career of robbery of princes, enamdars, zemindars, and huckdars† of all

* I have not space here, of course, to give a catalogue of the long series of public and private spoliations which characterised Lord Dalhousie's administration, and to give evidence of their influence on the rebellion; but the reader may find proofs enough of the correctness of my appreciation in the following authorities, perhaps even in the first I mention, which is the latest publication on the subject:—" The Empire in India," by Major Evans Bell; " Thoughts on the Policy of the Crown towards India," by J. M. Ludlow; " Rise and Progress of the Indian Mutiny: a full Examination of the alleged Causes of the Insurrection," by Montgomery Martin; " The Rebellion in India," by J. Norton; " The Sepoy Revolt," by H. Meade; " India: its Dangers Considered in 1856," by Col. Alves; Speech of Lord Ellenborough, July 11th, 1858—Hansard; Speech of Mr. Otway, M.P., April 28th, 1856—Hansard; " Civil Administration of Madras," by Mr. P. B. Smollett, M.P.; Evidence of Mr. J. Warden before the Colonization Committee of the House of Commons in 1858; " Enam Commission Unmasked," by R. Knight, of Bombay.

† *Vide* Dinker Rao's emphatic and repeated warning to the Government not to interfere with the Hucks of the people. He defines Hucks, or rights, as " Rights of property in land, or an office or employment, or any right in the largest sense of the English word." It has been said by two or three of our greatest living Anglo-Indian statesmen, that

descriptions, it could not but produce a state of moral anarchy among its subjects which would incline them to any outward and visible sign of their despair of justice: such as dacoitee, rebellion, &c.

In the present instance it was a sad proof of the extent to which our national conscience had been blunted by getting accustomed to the illegal and immoral spoliations of Lord Dalhousie, when we find our home authorities speaking of it as "a mark of especial favor" if the India Government does not rob its own friend's undoubted heir of his legitimate "inheritance!" There is no record of any Indian ruler who would have thought of "coveting his neighbour's goods" in such a case; never any who would not have admitted the right of his friend's "heir" as a matter of course; but our Anglo-Indian rulers, who are so anxious to convert "the Heathen" to Christianity, had absorbed such an amount of "their neighbours' goods" in the last few years that they were astonished at their own moderation if they "suffered" an adoption (of the legal heir), and spoke publicly of it as "a mark of especial favor!"

Finally, there was an implied menace in this phrase, not perhaps intended, but flowing naturally from the style of the secretary formed under the Dalhousie regime, who drafted the despatch;—there was this menace, that if the heir of the Dhar Rajah only obtained right and justice as "a mark of especial favor," the family "inheritance," held on such a precarious tenure, was not likely to last long, as annexation could not be indefi-

---

they had learnt more of India from Dinker Rao's conversation than they ever knew before. I think most Englishmen who could see Dinker Rao's "Memorandum on Indian Administration" would say as much of that.

nitely prevented by so fleeting a thing as "especial favor;" and so it proved.

Nevertheless, in spite of this one sentence, the intention of the above despatch was excellent, and its meaning was obvious. If you convict any of having been traitors, by all means punish them; but do not punish an innocent prince and people for a mere "inability to control mercenary troops," which they only shared with far more powerful neighbouring Native States, and even with the British Government itself (whose inability, in fact, *caused* theirs, and made it inevitable). Perhaps I may as well digress here to explain this fact, as the "inability to control its mercenary troops" is the only thing that has been proved, to this hour, against the State of Dhar.

CHAPTER III.

General circumstances which rendered every State in Central India unable to control its Mercenary Troops during the Summer of 1857.

THE time when the Dhar mutiny occurred, in the month of August, 1857, was the most critical period of that revolutionary movement in India, which we designated "the mutiny" because it was headed by the Native army, but which really was, in many parts of India, a national rebellion against a government of foreigners, whom the subject people felt to be aliens in everything from themselves,—aliens, not merely in blood, language, religion, and manners, but in interests and sympathies—aliens who habitually called them and treated them as "Niggers!"

This rebellion of the coloured races against us was of necessity begun by their army, because it was the only organised body, the only power, they had left in the State. One of the consequences of our system of uprooting their institutions, and treading in the dust their privileged classes, was, that an army raised from the inhabitants of the country should become the only representative of their interests, their feelings, and their force; and it was in consequence of this exclusive representation of, and intimate connection with, the inhabitants of the country, that, as I foretold in 1853,*

---

* Compare accounts of the outbreak at Meerut, &c., with extract from "India under a Bureaucracy," in Appendix B.

sooner or later the Native army was sure to sympathise with their countrymen* and revolt against us; and accordingly, in 1857, they did at length raise the fatal cry of "Death to the Englishmen!" which was echoed by a people in revolution wherever the army set the example.

At the commencement of this terrible rebellion, and for some months afterwards, our greatest danger was, that the Native princes might throw in their lot with the army and the people, and turn all India against us; and in some places, as in Rohilcund, Oude, Bundlecund, &c., the Native Chiefs did join the mutineers at the head of their clansmen. Had they done so generally, had they been merely passive, had not all the principal Native Princes and Chiefs, who had hitherto escaped annexation, exerted themselves actively on our side, it is certain that nothing could have saved our empire at that moment, and we should have had to reconquer India.

For some months before the date to which I refer, the conflagration in Upper India had been raging almost without a check, and constantly increasing in volume and intensity. The Sepoy mutiny had broken out in May; when it appeared that months of previous

---

* As examples of this sympathy I will mention three specific instances, and many more might be given. Before Oude was annexed, the regiments assembled in the North-West Provinces to carry out the annexation, united in sending a message to the King, that if he chose to resist they would not fight against him. Exactly the same message was sent to the Nizam by the Madras regiments on his frontier, when a report, spread under Lord Dalhousie's administration, that Hyderabad was to be annexed. The customary confiscations of our first Settlement Officers, after the annexation of Oude, produced 40,000 petitions against their proceedings from our Bengal Sepoys (probably recruits from Oude).

warning, and the general, notorious, often well-founded disaffection of our Native troops, had failed to induce the Government to take any precautions against the bursting of that volcano which was rocking under their feet, and emitting smoke and flames, and echoes of subterranean thunder, long before its sheet of fire rolled out.

From May to August the rebellion had been continually gaining strength, because Lord Canning's Government could not possibly help it. The handful of British troops in Northern India was so absorbed by Lord Dalhousie's latest annexations that there was almost no reliable force to oppose to the enemy, in a line of country stretching about 2,000 miles in length, from the Punjab to Pegu, and sometimes 1,000 miles in breadth, from the Himmalayahs to Candeish.

This particular one, among many causes of the mutiny, is not duly appreciated by the public. Before we annexed the Punjab we had a compact frontier of only 80 miles to guard, on the Sutlege, with no "little wars" in that quarter, and a British force stationed in healthy quarters in the North-West that held Upper India in perfect security. After we annexed the Punjab we undertook to guard a frontier of 800 miles in length, with a perpetual "little war" upon it, which has required the permanent cantonment of several British regiments in the "deadly valley" of Peshawar, besides an annual military expedition against the hill tribes from our garrisons on the Indus. (One of these expeditions is but just concluded as I write; the hill tribes have been fighting desperately, and we have had a considerable loss of officers and men.) However, the result of our withdrawal of British troops from Upper

India, to guard Lord Dalhousie's annexations,* was shortly this: Out of a total British force in the Bengal army of 18,815, rank and file, at the outbreak of the mutiny, 2,332 men were in Oude and Pegu, 11,351 in the Punjab and on its frontier, above 2,600 in neighbouring Stations acting as supports to the Punjab, and Lord Canning's Government had only 2,443 men left to defend all the rest of Upper and Lower Bengal and Central India; therefore, one of the things that tempted the Sepoys to revolt was, seeing the Supreme Government apparently at their mercy.

Considering this unpreparedness of the Government, it happened, as might have been expected, that in the beginning of the struggle, for above three months and a half, all our efforts seemed to end in still further exhausting our own strength and developing that of the enemy. Our measures of concentration were frustrated by our heavy loss of men. The climate, the long marches, the endless number of the rebels, the exposure to extreme heats and rains, in short, sickness and the sword, combined to empty our ranks as fast as we could close them up. Every day that the rebellion lasted increased the danger of seeing all India, and several warlike nations on its frontier, unite against us, and yet, after drawing every European that could be spared from other parts of India, our numerical inferiority to the enemy in Bengal remained as great as ever. At length a crisis arrived when, for a short time, our situation seemed so desperate that it is impossible to give an idea of it without recalling some details of the scene that met the eye towards the end of the month of

* *Vide* Remarks on the fallacy that "the Punjab saved India," in Appendix C.

August, 1857, and glancing successively at the isolated posts where small bodies of Englishmen still maintained our occupation of the country against a countless host of foes, including vast masses of trained soldiers, armed and equipped from our own arsenals, and abundantly supplied with our own English-made artillery. I allude not merely to such posts as Delhi, Agra, Cawnpore, and Lucknow, but also to stations nearer home, and in our notions comparatively close to Calcutta.

At Delhi, until the arrival of the last reinforcement from the Punjab, our small force nominally besieging the city, had really been itself besieged and nearly swept away, again and again, by those sorties of the Sepoys, which were interpreted in England as "*a proof of their weakness.*" As it was, after the above reinforcements, we had still to fight about ten times our own number of brave and disciplined troops, and had they possessed unity of action, the annihilation of the British force by simple overwhelming numbers could hardly have been doubted; perhaps, with all its heroism, our little Anglo-Sikh army owed as much to the intestine jealousies and divisions of the enemy as to its own valour; but as yet the divisions within the walls of Delhi were unknown to the world, and our force before the city seemed to be fatally overmatched.

Elsewhere the case seemed equally gloomy. At Agra our force had been shut up, after a defeat in the field, and was then closely blockaded and completely isolated and cut off. At Lucknow, also, after a defeat in the field, aggravated by the inestimable loss of Sir Henry Lawrence, our force was besieged in the Residency, and encumbered with helpless women and children, without casemates to afford any shelter, without numbers enough to man the walls, incessantly and fiercely attacked, and apparently without a chance of being saved, after the retreat of Havelock. At Cawnpore, Havelock, with only 700 bayonets, having lost more than half his force in the attempt to penetrate into Oude, had reported that he must retreat unless instant reinforcements could be promised him, as the famous Gwalior contingent of 8,000 men on one side, and a large force from Oude on the other, were rapidly advancing to unite in his rear. At Allahabad, Outram, when hurrying to relieve Havelock, had been suddenly obliged to halt, with his communications cut off, and his reinforcements taken away; for the revolt of the Dinapore and Bhagulpore regiments, added to the movements of Koor Sing's troops and the Ranegurgh battalions, &c., had so alarmed the civil authorities between Allahabad and Calcutta that they clutched desperately at every detachment on the road for local protection; and thus, out of 2,400 men destined to Outram's command, 1,800 were diverted at one time to flank operations. Meanwhile, the rapid fall of the Ganges had rendered the river line too precarious to be trusted, and it was necessary to clear 400 miles of the road by movable columns before troops could be forwarded by bullock train. Lastly, Calcutta was guarded by 1100 soldiers and some merchant seamen from the shipping in its port, with thousands of disarmed Sepoys at its gates, and tens of thousands of Budmashes, who might have armed them, within its walls.

And while such was the state of Bengal after every European that could be spared had been drawn from the minor governments, the prospect was little less gloomy in the other Presidencies. In Madras, symptoms of disaffection had appeared in the Native army, of which far too large a proportion were Mahommedans, and men lived in daily fear of seeing the whole Madras army swept into rebellion like a torrent, by the defection of Hyderabad. In Bombay, though Lord Elphinstone continued to put a bold face on the matter, perhaps no man was consciously in greater danger. While he continued to stamp out every spark of revolt in his own government, and contrived to despatch a moveable column to Central India (beyond Candeish, where Nana Sahib's agents were actively at work), he knew that the Bombay Native army was rotten to the core, that the Mahrattas were expecting the Peshwa, and the whole Deccan was in such a critical state, a spark might fire the train; and in his capital, with its population of three quarters of a million, including many thousands of bigoted hostile Mussulmen, he was obliged to trust his safety during a Mahommedan festival to a force of 300 Europeans, in the presence of 2,500 Sepoys who were known to be constantly plotting treason. Thus, Madras and Bombay were unsafe; Oude, Rohilcund, Bundlecund, the great North-West Provinces of Bengal were gone; except where, in the few posts I have mentioned, few and far between, British ensigns still showed above the waste of war, like rocks above a boiling surge, occasionally lost to sight in the tempest.

In fact, not only were Madras and Bombay unsafe, but only one thing was wanting to set all India in a blaze, and that seemed imminent, the defection of the Native Princes. Their armies, their people, even ladies of their zenana, and members of their families, urged them by every motive they could appeal to, to attack the hated foreigners at the head of their countrymen. It was felt that their opposition to the national movement deprived it of all moral sanction, and neutralised its temporary advantage of physical force. The body wanted a head to command it, and the most passionate efforts were made to gain over such princes as Scindiah, Holkar, the Nizam, the Banka Baee and others. They were promised empire; they were menaced with the extremities of popular fury; they were bitterly reproached with cowardly betrayal of their ancestors' fame, and their own and their people's interests; they were reminded how immensely we were outnumbered, how nearly we were exhausted; the mass of vulgar minds (as well English as Native) could not understand why Indian Princes, why all the most enlightened of the Indian race, should support the foreigners in such a crisis?

Yet statesmen now understand the reasons that decided Indian statesmen. *They* saw a doubtful present, with much to lose and little to win. *They* looked back to a stormy past. *They* put their trust in the future.*
After the rebellion, the system which preceded it could not be continued; the farmers of the revenue would be set aside, and the grasping " Company's Government" succeeded by a more just government of the Queen; it was good that the foreigners should have had a lesson from the rebellion, but it would be fatal if they were

* " Quod bello caput? unde jus auspicium que peteretur? Quam, si cuncta provenissent, sedem imperio legerent?"
" Regna bellaque per Gallias semper fuere, donec in nostrum jus concederetis."
" Quomodo sterilitatem aut nimios imbres et cetera naturæ mala, ita luxum vel avaritiam dominantium tolerate. Vitia erunt, donec homines: sed nequa hæc continua, et meliorum interventu pensantur."
—TACIT. HIST. lib. IV., cap. lxix., lxxiv.

mastered by it; they represented a higher civilisation than that of the rebels; if the Sepoys triumphed, India would revert to barbarism; its injuries would now be repaired if the foreigners remained; they had "sown "their wild oats," and would serve the country as well as themselves in the maturity of their empire; meanwhile the greater the danger, the greater would be the *gratitude** of the English to those who enabled them to surmount it. Therefore they took our side heartily, and every Native statesman was our stanch friend.

But the masses are not statesmen, and do not reason like them; so the majority of the combatants on both sides went on, vainly hoping or fearing that the Native princes would declare against us. And now the accumulation of disasters which I have described, was bruited over India, exaggerated, as usual, by Oriental hyperbole, yet enough without exaggeration to excite an ignorant, imaginative race almost to madness. It was for us a terrible moment! As at the darkest of the night, just before the dawn appears, so our danger reached its height in the month of August, 1857.

Was it possible at that moment for any State in Central India to escape injury from the hurricane of

---

* It provokes a bitter smile to remember the confident hopes and intense disappointment of many natives who did us "yeoman's service" at that time, sometimes at the risk of their lives for days together! I knew several such men who, after speculating on the honors and jaghires they must receive, if we could only weather the storm, found afterwards, that we, on the contrary, thought they were lucky to escape hanging. I think one of my friends died of his disappointment; several were in a worse position after than before the rebellion. One flagrant case was that of Holkar's minister. Next to Salar Jung, and Dinker Rao, Ramchunder Rao Martund was our most useful ally. By the malign influence of Col. Durand, both Maharajah and minister were at first rewarded by a semi-disgrace. Holkar has since had the Star of India: his minister has gained experience.

revolt then blowing over it, and to help seeing at least some of its troops carried away by the popular feeling? I say " some," because in no case did an entire army revolt. In every case some of the Native troops remained faithful. In our own case many of them shared all our dangers, and fought by our side from the beginning to the end of the war. Indeed, we could not have done without them; and, occasionally, as in the defence of Lucknow, their heroism in our cause was not to be surpassed.

It should not be forgotten about these Native troops that all of them were faithful a few years ago, in the days of Malcolm, Metcalf, &c.; and though the majority had become traitors in 1857, we have proofs that, even then, there was not only every shade of difference in their feelings, from the extreme of loyalty to the extreme of treason, but there was the strangest fluctuation between these extremes in the course of the rebellion. A minority was stanch throughout; a portion were always wavering; the majority, after hesitating for a shorter or longer period, generally turned against us on the impulse of the moment, from some unintentional provocation.

So it was in Dhar. The first symptoms of disaffection in the Dhar mercenaries occurred in July, just after the mutinies at Mhow and Indore, each about thirty miles off. But at that time the danger passed rapidly away, because the majority of Holkar's mutineers having marched off to Agra the day after the outbreak, when they found they could neither cajole nor frighten Holkar into joining them, and the Mhow troops having followed them, Holkar in a few days recovered his authority sufficiently to exert himself once more actively on the side of the English, and the example of course re-acted on Dhar. Its Government was again able to control its troops, and for some weeks longer it rendered essential service to the English cause.

In fact, when the Bombay moveable column reached Mhow on the 2nd of August, there was at first no reason to fear any further revolt in that neighbourhood. The natives were at first so awe struck by its presence, that it would have been easy to disarm any who were known to be doubtful or disaffected at Indore and Dhar, and to secure all the stations within a march or two of Mhow, as there was no force of the enemy that could oppose such measures within three or four times the distance; and the Natives expected this to be done almost every hour for several days after the arrival of the column.

But to their great surprise, the moveable column under Colonel Durand, became immoveable at Mhow for nearly three months, from the 2nd of August till the 20th of October; and then, as they recovered from their alarm, all the disaffected in the neighbourhood, instead of fearing us, began to think that we feared them; the old influences returned, the revolutionary propaganda became active again, and at the end of August, apparently from a sudden impulse, the Mussulman portion of the Dhar mercenaries broke into mutiny, and seized the fort of Dhar.

Yet these very Mussulmen had distinguished themselves by zeal, steadiness, and fidelity in the British service, not only before the rebellion, in campaigns against the Bheels, under Captains Johnston and Evans, for which they were most highly commended by those officers, and rewarded by the native Government, but even, for some time, during the rebellion, having served against the rebels to the last moment. Phenomena of this sort occurred so frequently at that time, that one acute observer and historian of the mutiny, Mr. Mead, adduced it as a proof that there could have been " no " plot, even among the Mussulmans, to rise against the " British Government,"* because the Native troops, in innumerable instances, refused at first to mutiny, and served us for awhile with signal fidelity against their own countrymen, although they afterwards joined them.

The fact is, that the gradual developement of the revolt among the uneducated classes will appear natural to those who consider the circumstances I have been describing. It was only the most highly educated and enlightened of the Natives who could persistently foresee and desire the return of British power. The ignorant, fanatical masses saw our authority overthrown, and its traces disappearing; they were not instructed enough to calculate that there would soon be a turn of the tide, which had been ebbing for nearly four months; they lived in an electrical atmosphere, charged with storms of public opinion; they listened to a popular frenzy of antipathy to the foreigners, and exultation at their disasters; they breathed an epidemic of rebellion, turning the brain of all the military classes, sooner or later, and hurrying them into the vortex, although they were often withheld for a time by old habits of discipline, or by the counteracting influence of their princes, whom they could not help respecting, though they could not understand their opposition to the national movement.

* " The Sepoy Revolt," page 170.

And this, which was the history of thousands in those days, was the history of these Dhar mercenaries. They were long restrained by their Native Court (sure to imitate the example of Holkar), long after the wave of mutiny, irresistibly attracting their sympathies, had reached and passed their garrison, and was flowing round it. Nevertheless, they did not join their countrymen; they continued to act against them; they did not break out until a circumstance occurred which was calculated to provoke their fanaticism to the utmost. On the 31st of August the British Agent at Bhopawur, recently assisted against the Amjhera rebels by a detachment of this very force, sent a "faquir" (Mussulman saint) to be confined at Dhar, when a part of the troops, of whom above three-fifths were Musselmen,[*] rose in tumult to the cry of "Deen!" (".the faith!") rescued the "faquir," and seized the fort of Dhar, which was not difficult in the surprise of a mutiny, as out of about a hundred men who formed the garrison at the time, thirty of the Konkanees (who remained faithful) were on guard over the treasury, while sixty of the Vellaitees, having their guard at the gates, of course opened them to the mutineers, who were their comrades and co-religionists.

---

[*] The State had then in its service 339 Mussulmen, 100 Poorbeah Sepoys, 50 Bundelas, and 50 Konkanees, total 539 men. The two last corps, making together 100 men, were employed by the Native Government, as the most trusted portion of its troops, for treasure, city, and palace guards, and owing to their stanchness throughout the mutiny, they were retained at Dhar, in our service, after our confiscation of the State. But nothing could be more illogical than for us to take a portion of the Dhar troops into the British service, because they had always obeyed the Native Government, and then to punish the Native Government because another portion of its troops disobeyed and mutinied against it.

Such were the public and private circumstances under which the mercenary troops of Dhar threw off the control of its Government; and I am sure that any impartial person would indorse the verdict of the Home Government when Lord Stanley presided over it, that " we cannot consistently punish this or any other weak " state for its inability to control its troops, when it " was patent to the whole world that the more powerful " States of Gwalior and Indore, and even the British " Government itself, were unable to control theirs."

CHAPTER IV.

Two Special Circumstances which made the State of Dhar more unable than other States to control its Mercenary Troops.

I HAVE shown that the "inability to control their " mercenary troops" was common to every State in Central India, from the British Government downwards, during the summer of 1857; but there were special circumstances which increased this inability in the case of Dhar, arising from the character and conduct of the British functionary, Colonel Durand, who was appointed to supply the place of Sir Robert Hamilton, during his temporary absence in England, as Resident at Indore, and chief political agent in Malwa.

I must pause here for a moment to say, that one of the most indefensible acts of our Indian Government is to appoint men to an office of this sort who are known to be unfit for it, through their temper or their antipathy to the Natives. I am sorry to say it appears that Government never scruples to do this, whatever misery and mischief it may cause to Native princes and people, if the officials in question have interest enough to back their claim to the appointment, or if the government wishes to get them out of their previous situation to promote somebody in their place. The result is, that the despotism of some of our Indian " Politicals " is hardly credible; nor would it ever become known, as the unfortunate Native princes themselves are prevented from corresponding with England, if it did not almost invariably happen that some Englishman, involuntarily connected with these transactions as a public servant, is so shocked by the oppression at which he is unwillingly compelled to assist, that he sends home, at the least, a private protest to his friends, which finds its way to other parties, and very often, at the risk of ruining his own prospects for life, appeals openly to the government, or to the public, on behalf of our victims. This was generally the case, to the credit of our countrymen be it spoken, even under the administration of Lord Dalhousie, when any man who ventured to oppose such proceedings was disgraced without mercy: but such revelations were fruitless then, owing to the indifference of the English people to Indian questions, and to this day the evil has never been remedied.

"What mischief is often done by Residents," says Mr. Ludlow; "how they gall and crush the Native
" princes, can hardly be said in too vivid terms. Lord
" Hasting's portrait of them in 1814 is true yet to the
" life:—Instead, said his Lordship, of acting in the
" character of ambassador, he (the Resident) assumes
" the functions of a dictator; interferes in all their
" private concerns; countenances refractory subjects
" against them; and makes the most ostentatious
" exhibition of this exercise of authority. To secure
" himself the support of our government he urges
" some interest which, under the colour thrown upon
" it by him, is strenuously taken up by our council,
" and the government identifies itself with the Resi-
" dent, not only on the single point, but on the

" whole tenor of his conduct." Mr. Ludlow adds:
" The feelings of the Chiefs and Durbars towards our
" politicals and their underlings are well described by
" one on the spot as those of ' terror.' "*

Formerly our political agents in India, men of persuasive manners and enlightened, just views, exercised an immense moral influence over the Native States of India;† but "we have lost our *moral* hold over the " passions and prejudices of India," as Major Bell observes,‡ by the arrogance, the impatience of contradiction, the contempt for Native arguments, and the disposition to appeal immediately to force, which characterises our modern negociators, and latterly, our " Indian " diplomacy has not only been meddling, overbearing, " and rapacious, but has been eminently unsuccessful " in securing its avowed objects, and dangerous and " disadvantageous in the results which it has actually " produced." " Even one of the best of modern Resi-" dents," says Major Bell, and my experience confirms this observation, one of those most anxious for the improvement of Native administration, " would consider " any reform to be dearly purchased by any measure " that should render the Native prince and his ministers " less dependent on the Resident." . . . " The fact is," he adds, " that according to the accepted traditional " language of our Indian political officers, all consulta-" tions at a Native court, to which the Resident is not " privy, and of which he has not expressed his approval,

* " Thoughts on the policy of the Crown towards India," pages 178, 179.

† Having illustrated this point in a memoir of my late friend Sir Claude Wade, contributed to the " Journal of the Royal Asiatic Society," I beg to refer to some extracts from that paper, in Appendix C.

‡ " The Empire in India," pages 391, 392, also 310, 311.

" are called *intrigues*." " Every man, whatever his rank
" may be, who has access to the prince or his minister,
" and who is supposed to have an opinion of his own,
" or to give advice contrary to that of the Resident, is
" said to be 'a man of an intriguing and turbulent
" disposition.'"

Such being the normal character of our political agents in India, let the reader conceive how every defect in that character would be aggravated by the training they received under Lord Dalhousie, when not only mis-statement and misrepresentation was habitually and unscrupulously resorted to, to strip princes or private landholders of their property; not only moral torture— bullying, humiliation, and actual privation—was pitilessly applied to the victims of our rapacity, to enforce their silence and submission, but when the head and model of the official corps, the Governor-General himself set the example of speaking to the Native Sovereigns of India, as if too much despotism had made him mad —for Lord Dalhousie, in the course of bullying the Nizam into a surrender of his richest provinces, actually likened him, in a letter full " of unworthy invective " and sarcasm, to '*the dust under his feet!*'"* Such being the master, supported by the Court, the Government, and the *Times* at home, we may imagine what were his men! and of all our political officers formed in the Dalhousie school, perhaps Colonel Durand

* These were the words of a Member of Parliament, of irreproachable character, and who has held a high official position in this country, after reading the original letter in the Archives of Hyderabad.—*Vide* " Quarterly Review " for July, 1858, page 265. I hear that " *the dust under his feet* " has suddenly recollected inconveniently for us, that he is a sovereign prince, and has public engagements as such; including a Treaty, that interferes with our intention of comfortably digesting Mysore, " *en famille !*"

was its most exact representative. His temper is as well-known here as it is in India. His antipathy to the Natives is so marked as to prevent their holding *voluntarily* any intercourse with him, except what official business renders unavoidable. He had got into difficulties in every political appointment he held before he was appointed to act in Sir Robert Hamilton's absence as Resident at Indore (by a curious coincidence the very man who began the revolt there, was a State prisoner whom Colonel Durand had formerly patronized as a pretender to the musnud of Bhopal). He was maintained in that appointment after writing, at the very crisis of our fate, such an intemperate letter* to the noble and generous Holkar, who had freely risked his life in our cause,† as might have precipitated another man into hostility, and this in the height of the revolution fever, when Holkar might any day have rallied a hundred

---

* For which he was reprimanded by Lord Elphinstone's Government.

† Here is an extract from the high authority I have just quoted, in the " Quarterly Review " of July, 1858 :—" The education of Holkar " from his childhood had been confided to the superintendence of a " man who treated the natives of India with justice and kindness, and " who ventured to respect the rights and feelings even of a ' nigger.' " The lessons taught by Sir Robert Hamilton, and by a visit to " Bombay, where he had been received by Lord Elphinstone, had not " been thrown away. When the revolting regiments called out to him, " on his refusing to lead them against the English, ' What would your " ' great ancestor have done at such a moment?' he boldly replied, " ' That I cannot say; but I know what he would not have done—he " ' would not have joined the murderers of women and children !' His " life, like that of Scindiah's, was threatened by the mutineers; but " he unflinchingly persevered in his fidelity to us, saved the lives of " many Christian families by receiving them in his palace, and rescued " those who had fallen into the hands of hostile chiefs. The return we " have made to him for these great services has been to insult him in " his capital, to demand the surrender of his near relatives as traitors, " and to hang summarily and with scarcely the form of, we will not " say a trial, but an inquiry, his own subjects !"

thousand Mahrattas to his standard, and have turned the scale against us.

Here, lest I should be suspected of exaggerating the defects of Colonel Durand's temper and manners, I refer the reader to an article on his appointment to the post of Foreign Secretary in India, extracted from one of the most respectable local journals (a journal repeatedly quoted in support of its opinions by the Home Government), viz., the *Times of India*,* which article, though complimentary to Colonel Durand, explains his unfitness for such an office in language which is known to be true by every diplomatist in India, as well as by the government which sanctioned his appointment.

I must, however, particularly notice one instance of Colonel Durand's indulgence of temper, because it gives a clue to the secret history of this Dhar case. The reader, who will refer to the first mild protest of Sir Robert Hamilton, on July 5th, 1858,† against anything that might " bear the semblance of injustice or plunder," in our appropriating the Dhar treasure as prize money, may be astonished at the truculent spirit in which Colonel Durand replied to him. Among other bitter taunts on his change of opinions, his " suppression," " distortion," and " evasion of important facts," Colonel Durand (strong in the favour of the Governor-General) did not scruple to upbraid a superior officer, of such well known respectability and experience as Sir Robert Hamilton, with " the spurious tenderness which prefers " that the reality of injustice be inflicted on British " troops, rather than run the risk that the semblance

---

* *Vide* Appendix D.

† Parliamentary Paper, No. 30, of 1861, pages 14, 15, and *infra* pages 17 to 27.

" of injustice, however illusory and conjured up on
" false premises and *ad misericordiam* arguments, be
" alleged by those who sought the destruction of our
" troops and the humiliation of our power, and by such
" as accept their bias."

Perhaps, on looking back to Sir Robert Hamilton's
" remonstrance," as the Supreme Government styled
the above-mentioned dispatch,* the reader may wonder
how such a very temperate statement could provoke
such an intemperate reply. The fact is, that (evidently
without intending to attack him, or then knowing the
extent of his culpability) Sir Robert Hamilton had
incidentally raised a question which gravely compromised Colonel Durand, and made him personally
responsible for the disorders which had occurred
in the State of Dhar. Therefore it is that Colonel
Durand was so angry at the least remonstrance;
therefore it is that he exhibited such malignity
against the State of Dhar, bringing forward against
it, in default of anything substantial, all the old
gossip and false charges which had already been
answered or explained before he wrote this minute
of July 26th, 1858,† because it was his interest to
throw the blame on the Dhar Government in order
to avert it from himself. When anarchy, intrigue, and
triumphant mutiny in Dhar could be traced to his own
successive faults, he found it necessary to make a scapegoat of the Dhar Durbar, to save his own reputation;
and as I exonerate the State of Dhar, by going over
every separate charge against it, I shall show that

---

* Parliamentary Paper, No. 30, of 1861, page 16.

† Parliamentary Paper, No. 30, of 1861, pages 17 to 27.

Colonel Durand repeatedly and signally failed to do his duty as a political agent.

The sentences in Sir Robert Hamilton's letter which put Colonel Durand on his defence were these:—After referring to the death of the late Rajah (which happened on May 23rd, 1857), and the recognition of his adopted heir, the letter continues, para. 4, " the administration " under a Regency was barely formed when the mutiny " broke out." And para. 5, "Intimation of the recog- " nition was made to the Durbar on the 28th of Septem- " ber, 1857, but the Khillut of investiture was not then " (nor has it yet been) sent." (This was written July 5th, 1858). Let it be observed that Sir Robert did not say, " Colonel Durand left the State without a head for " five months together." He did perhaps imply this; but at any rate he did not say, nor imply, that "Colonel Durand broke up the administration, and " threw the local authorities into a state of anarchy; " leaving the public servants, civil and military, without " any responsible person to look to." Sir Robert did not say this (though I shall), and yet Colonel Durand cried out as if he was so tender on that point, that not merely he could not bear to be touched on it, but he could not bear to see any one approach who might touch it. Now, before I deal with his mis-statements about the Minister "*with the support of the Government of* "*India at his back!*" let me say a few words on the point of the indefinite delay of "investiture"—of that *public act of recognition* which Colonel Durand, as an old political agent, knew perfectly well to be necessary, not merely as a form of law, but as a visible matter of fact, to assure the native community that the succession of the young Rajah was recognized by the British Government. He admits it himself when it suits his argument. For instance, after asserting in his minute, para. 3, that the Durbar was not kept in suspense, but was very quickly informed of our recognition of the young Rajah, he says, at para. 22, " that though his adoption and " succession had been officially recognized, the sealing " act, viz., the investiture by conferring a Khillut on " the part of the Government of India had not been " carried into effect; strictly speaking, therefore, we " had not put the minor on the Guddee (throne)."

This "*sealing act*," therefore, was indefinitely postponed; and, with the exception of a mere verbal promise to the Dhar Vakeel, about ten days or a fortnight after the late Rajah's death, that is, about the end of May or beginning of June, 1857, there was not, even in private, any official recognition of the young Rajah until the 1st of October, when a letter was at length sent to him, announcing the Governor General's sanction of his succession. The above verbal promise was obtained by telegraph, and the permission to carry it into execution ought also to have been obtained by telegraph, for there never was a time when delay was so dangerous. The revolt of the Malwa Contingent in the Jowerah district, on the 2nd of June, and the mutiny at Neemuch a few days after, had spread alarm through all the chief towns in Malwa; and if ever a strong administration was needed in the world, it was so at that moment in the States of Central India; therefore a public recognition of the successor, a composition of the Regency, and an organisation of the Government was a matter of the most pressing necessity in Dhar at that crisis.

But I have already described the dictatorship usurped

by our political agents in the Native courts, and the people look to these functionaries to settle everything, especially in the case of a minority; they look to them, not merely in a petty state like Dhar, but in the most powerful of Native States, such as those of Scindiah and Holkar, to publicly declare a successor, to compose a Regency (of which they themselves are the real heads), to appoint or confirm every official, and to decide upon the appropriation of every pound of revenue; well knowing that every arrangement made without their previous sanction is sure to be disallowed and reversed.

It may be said, admitting all this, the only thing Colonel Durand could do at first was to publicly recognise the adoption, and thus settle the succession in the eyes of the people; and though he was to blame for not doing this, the other arrangements, such as composing the Regency, could not be made without inquiry and consideration, involving some little time and trouble; as the sudden death of the late prince, who governed as well as reigned, in the flower of his age, had taken every one by surprise, and, moreover, had plunged his family into such deep grief, that it would not have been decorous to force the Court to transact business for a month after the funeral (which took place on June 6th), as in fact they did not; and before that time Colonel Durand was in full flight for Hosunghabad, having been driven from Indore, in the opposite direction from Dhar, on the 1st of July.

However, I can show that this short absence of Colonel Durand (he was back at Mhow on the 2nd of August) does not in the least diminish his responsibility, because a Regency was composed, with British official sanction, during Colonel Durand's absence, and the very first thing he did on his return was to upset this arrangement, *without making any other in lieu of it*, so that he literally kept the State without any recognised head or authorised government for five months together, until our troops entered it, and he recommended its confiscation. This is a grave charge, but I am about to produce documentary evidence to prove it.

Very soon after the late Rajah's death, Colonel Durand wrote to Captain Hutchinson as follows:—" Pending " final arrangements for the administration of the Dhar " Principality, you will be responsible for the conduct " of affairs, and the maintenance of peace and order;" and he added that he wished him to take advantage of the advice of Bappoo Sahib, the Rajah of Dewass, a Puar himself, and a confidential friend of the late Jeswunt Rao Puar, who was about to pay a visit of condolence to the family.*

This visit, for reasons above stated, could not be paid till July; and at that date the Dewass Rajah on visiting Dhar, found several candidates for the Regency, viz., the two Ranees, Bheem Rao Bhonsla (brother of the elder Ranee), and the experienced old minister Ramchunder Rao Bapojee, who had been eleven years out of office because he incurred the late Rajah's displeasure, but who was a protegé of the English, enjoyed a jaghire under their guarantee, and had a tolerable knowledge of the English language. For these reasons, although the Ranee naturally wished her brother to be chosen, and several officers of state demurred to the selection of the old minister, the Dewass Rajah persuaded them to select at such a crisis, a person notoriously devoted

* Parliamentary Paper, No. 200, of 1859, page 7.

to the English interest, and, therefore, after communicating with Captain Hutchinson and obtaining his consent, Bappoo Sahib formally appointed the old minister on the 22nd of July, 1857, and he had but just got the administration into working order when Colonel Durand returned. Will it be believed that one of Colonel Durand's first acts on arriving at Mhow, was to cancel this appointment! Within four days of his return, the following note, accompanying an official despatch of the same tenor and date, was sent by Captain Hutchinson to the Dhar Vakeel:—

" To Raghonaut Narain, Vakeel of the Dhar State,
" Bhopawur Agency.

" SIR,
" With reference to the appointment of the
" Dewan, I beg to inform you that on my reporting
" the same to Colonel Durand, the Offg. Agent Govr.-
" Genl., he informed me that he had distinctly in-
" structed His Highness, Bappoo Sahib, through the
" Durbar Vakeel, that *no appointment* was to be made
" without *his* sanction and approval. You ought to
" have informed me of this, for you cannot bring for-
" ward my approval to the appointment, when Colonel
" Durand so distinctly gave his orders on the subject.

" I am, &c.,
" D. A. R. E. HUTCHINSON,
" Bheel Agent and Pol. Assist.

" Mhow, 6th August, 1857."

The official despatch was as follows:—

Translation of a Perwanah from Captain Hutchinson, Bheel Agent and Political Assistant, to Raghonaut Narain, Vakeel of Dhar, dated 6th of August, 1857.

" With reference to your private letter regarding the
" appointment of the Dewan, I beg to inform you that
" on my communicating the same to the Offg. Agent
" Govr.-General, I was directed to intimate that no
" appointment can be made without his sanction, and
" the Dhar Durbar was distinctly ordered on the
" subject. You are therefore desired to inform me
" what has taken place."

Now be it remembered that this appointment had been made as a matter of necessity, during Colonel Durand's absence for an indefinite period, without the least intention of offending or slighting him, but to supply, in critical and dangerous circumstances, a pressing want of the State and the afflicted family,* and supply it in the manner most conducive to English interests. Yet, to show his resentment for this, at least well-meant act, Colonel Durand, at one blow, completely paralysed and dissolved the so-called Regency; leaving the State from that day forward, until he thought it ripe for confiscation, without any supreme controlling authority, backed by the support of the Government of India: which I have shown to be

---

* The younger Ranee died broken-hearted, five months after her husband, aged 20; and the elder Ranee, who died in 1860, at the age of 32, may be said to have been worried to death by our treatment of her.

necessary now in all the Native States, to keep the Officers of State in subordination, to command their respect and obedience, and to prevent a conflict of authority in the Durbar itself, and in the civil and military services under it. The result was, of course, immediate intrigue and factions, and the enlistment of more mercenary troops by the rival parties to strengthen themselves against each other.

Sir Robert Hamilton spoke with intense disgust in his minute of such a scramble for power in Dhar at such a time;* but, perhaps, he would have been more lenient to a petty state of India if he had been more behind the scenes in his own country. Those who witnessed the intrigues which were the scandal of London in February, 1855, and which kept the country for days without a government, at the most alarming crisis of the Crimean war, drew the moral then, not for India but for England, that no amount of public danger, and no prospect of the country's good, can induce ambitious politicians to forego their rivalries, and postpone their personal pretensions, as long as they can hope to indulge their selfishness with impunity; and if Sir Robert Hamilton will look over a file of the *Times* newspaper at that period, he will find the reckless selfishness of our aristocracy denounced in far stronger language than he himself applied to the aristocracy of Dhar.

However, I do not mean to defend such conduct. I only say it was natural for factions to arise when Colonel Durand thus paralysed the so-called Regency, and left the government without a head; and accordingly, from the day when he cancelled the above appointment, the poor Ranees were surrounded with

* Parliamentary Paper, No. 30, of 1861, page 15.

insurmountable difficulties, and the administration of Dhar fell into confusion. In vain did the unfortunate minister, who found himself disgraced and impotent, without being nominally dismissed (for the Ranees and minor Rajah could not appoint any one in his room without the sanction of Colonel Durand), in vain did he write repeatedly to Colonel Durand, and endeavour to prove his zeal by giving prompt information to the Vakeels at Bhopawur and Mhow. Colonel Durand never deigned to answer or even acknowledge his letters, or take any notice of him again, until the Durbar of October 26th, when he bullied him to his heart's content,* and told him that all the responsibility for what had happened should fall on him.†

It must, however, be obvious to the reader of the foregoing statement, that the first and greatest of the special causes which produced the inability of the Dhar State "to control its mercenary troops," was Colonel Durand's complete disorganisation of its Government and break up of the Regency, by wantonly cancelling the minister's appointment, and thus leaving the Durbar in a state of anarchy, without either a recognised ruler of the State, or a chief political authority holding unreserved personal communication with himself, and depending on his advice and support; *in flagrant violation of the duties prescribed to him as a resident and political agent by well known circular orders of*

* Parliamentary Paper, No. 30, of 1861; page 22, para. 29, 30; and page 34, para. 27.

† Accordingly, after the siege he was arrested and placed in confinement, and had the simplicity to go on for months petitioning that he might be brought to trial, declaring his innocence, and wondering whether he was suspected of corresponding with the King of Delhi, or what was the specific charge against him. *Le pauvre homme!*

Government, which ought to have been familiar to him from practice and experience, and which enjoined him to remember that he was "deputed as the representative " of the friendship, as well as of the power, of the " British Government."*

Yet so confident was he that the Supreme Government would take for granted anything he said, and would not under any circumstances enquire into the facts, in spite of the strongest presumptive evidence that he had mis-stated them, that he did not hesitate to make assertions in his minute which are flatly contradicted by the documents I have cited; such as this, for instance, para. 4: "In composing the Regency, the minister " selected was the only new coadjutor. The adminis-" tration of the State continued in its usual track, and " was in as uninterrupted and undisturbed action after " as it had been before the death of the late Rajah;" and again at para. 20, where he says, that if the minister had found any reason to complain of faction, "*with the* " *support of the Government of India at his back* (!) he " would assuredly have been quick enough in making " such representations, had there been grounds." I must leave the reader to qualify these assertions as they deserve, merely remarking that this style of reckless misrepresentation is common to every pro-annexation minute I have read for the last fifteen years.

But there was another special cause for the inability of the Dhar State to control its mercenary troops, besides Colonel Durand's break-up of the Regency, and that was his refusal to give the Native Government that armed help which it had always willingly afforded us,

---

* These noble instructions, issued by Lord Ellenborough, are dated April 26th, 1842.

as long as its troops would obey orders, and often to our signal relief and advantage,—help which we were bound by Treaty, by the obligation of gratitude, and by the dictates of ordinary prudence, to give in our turn, because it was pressingly demanded by the Native Government at times when it would have been easy to restore its authority, always exerted in our favour, and to prevent the necessity of undertaking a regular siege of the fort. This refusal was the ruin of the State, and I must show that the attempts to justify it are unsuccessful.

I have already explained the mischievous effects of Colonel Durand's stopping the moveable column at the fort of Mhow, instead of marching only ten miles further to re-occupy the Residency at Indore, which would have produced the best moral effect on Western Malwa, and material effect too, if he had simultaneously secured the neighbouring stations.

The reason publicly given for this halt at the time, was, that the Residency at Indore having been much injured in the mutiny of the 1st of July, Colonel Durand would wait at Mhow till it was repaired;* but the Natives could not believe that a "moveable column" dispatched to re-occupy one of the most important stations and centres of influence in India, should be halted before it reached its destination, merely because the acting Resident did not think the old house quite comfortable enough yet to accommodate him. And if they did not believe this reason at first, still less did they believe it when they saw the "moveable column" remain immoveable for nearly three months, at the strong fort of Mhow, although the longer its immobility lasted, the

---

* *Vide* the *Bombay Times* of August 15th, 1857.

greater of course became the audacity and enterprise of all the rebels in Malwa, who, finding that a "moveable "column," under Colonel Durand, did not prevent *their* moving where they liked, and doing what they pleased, gradually congregated in his neighbourhood as they were driven out of other parts, for we were nowhere immoveable except at Mhow, until they at length proceeded to the outrages at Bhopawar and Sirdapore, on the 10th of October, which we visited on the head of the boy Rajah of Dhar. Even then Colonel Durand's patience was not exhausted; even then he took ten days more to consider of it before he made up his mind to set the "moveable column" in motion again; but as he was then obliged to give some better reason for its immobility, which had produced such serious consequences, than waiting for carpenters' and upholsterers' work at Indore, he declared that the state of the weather and muddiness of the roads had prevented his moving before the 20th of October.*

Now, those who remember the marches that were being made elsewhere by Europeans and Natives during the same period, especially the marches of Greathead's moveable column, which will never be forgotten in Indian history, will naturally ask why Colonel Durand should have been more "fettered by the rains" than any other commander. For no one else was "fettered;" the fall of Delhi had been preluded by the wonderful marching and fighting of Nicholson towards the end of August; immediately after its fall, in September, Wilson organised and started Greathead's moveable column, which, after incessant marching and fighting for several

* Para. 13 of Minute, Parliamentary Paper, No. 30, of 1861, page 19.

weeks, had wound up by the extraordinary forced march to Agra, and rout of the Indore brigade at that place, on the 10th of October, which was one of the most brilliant feats of arms during the war; after which Greathead, instead of "patiently awaiting finer weather," like Colonel Durand, had forthwith started again for Cawnpore, where his arrival greatly contributed to the success of Sir Colin's first campaign.

Yet Colonel Durand expects us to believe that all the while, when other moveable columns, and the enemy in his neighbourhood, could march freely enough, the weather prevented his moving! The excuse is not merely inadmissible, but I will show, from two other assertions that he makes in the same breath, in the same paragraph, that it is almost absurd. He says, to illustrate his "compulsory inaction" from wet weather, that "on the 19th of September he received a press-"ing message from Holkar's minister to march upon "Indore;" and that from another quarter he learnt that there was to be an insurrection at Indore, on "the "Dusserah, the 28th of September." Now I must notice the fact that the Dusserah begins on the 19th of September, corresponding with the 1st of the Native month (Auswin), because this date has a curious bearing on the facts he has connected with it. The commencement of the festival of Dusserah, or Doorga-Pooja, is associated in men's minds with the *cessation of the rains*, as any one who knows Malwa can bear witness; the rains are generally considered to have ceased before the festival begins, on the 19th of September, and I am informed positively that they had done so in that year, 1857, and yet Colonel Durand did not move for a month longer! With regard to the alleged "pressing "message to march upon Indore," it must be recollected that Colonel Durand had a "moveable column," strong in cavalry, including English cavalry, and artillery, with a larger proportion of British infantry than often fell to the lot of "moveable columns" in those days, and transport enough to carry every man of that valuable force to the field, if they could not walk over the ten miles of good macadamised road from Mhow to Indore; in fact he had a "moveable column" strong enough for any service that could be required in Malwa; and yet he says that he received this "pressing message" from Indore, but did not move for a month afterwards! Of course the pressing message is either an invention or a delusion, for although there were then plots and disaffection at Indore, as there were at Bombay, they were not half so dangerous at the former place. At Bombay, the great majority of the troops were disaffected; at Indore it was no longer so, it was just the reverse; and when the Dusserah came, Holkar was "prepared for any emergency." I repeat that, from the day the bulk of the mutineers marched away to Agra, Holkar had not only been recovering his authority, but using it with great effect on our side, of which frequent notices occur in the Bombay journals of that period.

It is evident from the above enquiry that "the "rains" were not a valid excuse for Colonel Durand's halting the moveable column from the 2nd of August to the 20th of October, and considering what brave Lord Elphinstone had risked by sparing such a force at such a time* it may be imagined that some disappoint-

---

* "The whole of Khandeish, the Deccan, and Southern Mahratta "country were ripe for rebellion at any moment."—"Western India

ment was felt at Bombay, at seeing the rebels allowed to collect at their leisure, and plunder and burn within easy reach of the Bombay column; and that Colonel Durand may remember "pressing messages" from other quarters than Indore, when he admits "the animad-"versions cast upon our unaccountable inaction."* For the very meaning and object of a "moveable "column" is to seek out and disperse danger within a given sphere of operations, and as all the enemy's regular troops, the really formidable brigades of Gwalior, Indore, and Mhow, had left the country, the force entrusted to Colonel Durand was amply sufficient for the purpose when he reached Malwa, though his long and (in his own phrase) "unaccountable inaction" for nearly three months, allowed dangers to gather, to grow, and spread, until when he did move at last, the rebel head raised at Dhar might have made a serious resistance, and certainly would have done so if the Native Court had joined it, and given it that moral and quasi-legal support, the want of which always unnerved the rebels—the siege of Dhar would have been a different story if the Ranee had joined her troops, like the Ranee of Jhansi, instead of always opposing them.

But the "rains" were not Colonel Durand's only excuse for his "unaccountable inaction" at Mhow. He implies that the force of the enemy (though delay in

" has been loyal only because it has been held down by artillery; a
" conspiracy all but universal having bound together the influential
" classes of the Mofussil above the Ghauts."—" Not fewer than 500
" pieces of concealed ordnance were discovered in the Southern
" Mahratta country alone."—*Vide* preface to " Inam Commission Un-
" masked," by Mr. R. Knight, editor of the *Bombay Times*.

* Para. 14 of Minute, Parliamentary Paper, No. 30, of 1861, page 19.

attacking was a sure way to increase it), and the weakness of his column were also considerations "that gave " him pause." Now, what he says on both these points is so marked by exaggeration, that it looks as if his mind had been off its balance, and under some delusion, at this period.

I have before said that his column was not weak—strength is, of course, a relative term—but his force was amply strong enough to dispose of all the rebels, or "rabble," for that would really be a more appropriate term for the enemies he had to disperse, in Malwa. He makes a formidable parade of these enemies in his minute;* like the roll-call in the "Iliad" before the fighting begins; but he must also have invoked the Muses before he penned such a description of "the " state of affairs *around* Mhow!" for he actually includes in affairs "around Mhow," insurrections in Bundelcund and south of it, hundreds of miles off, where the people could no more dream of reaching him than he ever dreamt of reaching them! and, after dwelling upon the Shahzadar at Mundesor, and estimating his force as "at least 20,000 men by the end of August" (the date of the Dhar mutiny), he describes as one of the dangers " around Mhow" a petty local outbreak beyond Malwa, never likely to enter it, and which *had been put down before the end of August* in Nimawur! He also includes in dangers "around Mhow," that the Bheels had began to plunder and infest the Bombay road; but these Bheels, in Candeish, were at least fifty miles south of the Nerbudda, and never likely to cross it, for they are mere savage highwaymen, never leaving their hill and jungle to fight in the open field; and, on this

* Para. 7.

occasion, as they had broken out in Holkar's territory near Sindwa, he had sent his troops to co-operate with the Bheel corps, under Captain Cumming, against them. In short, on analysing Colonel Durand's own statement, we find no residuum of hostile force "around "Mhow," or anywhere near it, at the date of the Dhar mutiny, except the Shahzada at Mundesor and he was at least 120 miles off; a good many marches, according to Colonel Durand's computation, almost enough to allow our "moveable column" to march to Dhar and back again, twice over, before he could arrive, even if he had been inclined to do so. But he knew better; he never thought of such a thing; he had as much respect for our column as Colonel Durand had for his "rabble," and a good deal more reason for it! Even if he could have persuaded the bulk of his men, who came from Scindiah's adjoining districts, to march away from their own locality, which was not likely, such raw undisciplined levies, and all the plunderers and freebooters who had joined them, would have stood about as much chance as a herd of cattle attacking lions, if they had ventured to attack a British column, well furnished in all arms, perfect in discipline, and numbering in its ranks several hundreds of English soldiers! I repeat that if Colonel Durand really believed such a thing possible, his mind must have been off its balance at this period.

However, having thus shown that his "inaction" at the time of the Dhar mutiny *was* "unaccountable," and not justified either by the weather or by the strength of any hostile force in his neighbourhood, I will now describe the circumstances under which his refusal of the Dhar Government's urgent demand for help proved the ruin of the Native State.

The first occasion was on the mutiny of August 31st, when the Mussulmen seized the fort of Dhar. Immediate explanation of this event was forwarded by the Durbar to Captain Hutchinson at Bhopawar, and to Colonel Durand at Mhow, giving, in addition to the facts I have before stated, a number of other details, as to what the fort contained of treasure, grain, ammunition, and guns, with the state of the guns, &c., and praying for a detachment of the British force to punish the mutineers, of whom there were probably less than 300 irretrievably committed at first; so that if Colonel Durand had sent a detachment at once, with a couple of guns, and by the help of his elephants and camels, the European infantry and the baggage could have been protected from the wet, he might easily, by the help of the Native Government, have crushed this mutiny in the bud, though from his delay to act, in seven week's time it had attracted about 2,000 rebels to garrison the fort and take the field against us. In war, time is invaluable!

But not only was this first application of the Dhar Government refused; such applications were repeatedly refused, and silenced for a time. As the poor Ranee said, in her letter to the Governor-General,[*] of May 1st, 1858—"From the day the Wellaitees seized the " fort, constant applications for assistance were sub- " mitted to the British authorities. The importunity " seemed at last to be so distasteful, that even a reference

[*] The only notice ever taken by the Government of this touching and truthful appeal, was a curt intimation, above three months after its receipt, that it must be transmitted through the official channel of the " Governor-General's agency for Central India." It will be found in the annexures to Sir R. Hamilton's second despatch. Parliamentary Paper, No. 30, of 1861, page 36, para. 37, and page 42, annexure No. 11.

" to the subject was deemed offensive." Nevertheless, although Colonel Durand adhered to his "unac-
" countable inaction," there are at least three proofs that at this time he considered the explanation of the mutiny by the Dhar Government satisfactory.

1st. He did not ask for any further explanation, which he certainly would have done if he suspected the Durbar of any connivance with the mutineers.

2nd. He endorsed the comments of Capt. Hutchinson on this mutiny. Captain Hutchinson having said on the 1st of September—"The mercenaries of Dhar and " Amjhera are out of the control of their respective " chiefs," Colonel Durand forwarded his report, on the 3rd of September, with the remark—"The impotence " of every chief, great or small, to control their levies " is a normal feature of the state of armed anarchy " which afflicts the country."*

3rd. A month afterwards, on the 1st of October, he forwarded to the Dhar Durbar the Khareeta, giving the sanction of the Supreme Government to the adoption of the young Rajah,† which he could not have done if during the whole previous month he had considered the Durbar to be traitors.

Therefore he admitted the Durbar's explanation of the mutiny, and seizure of the fort, to be satisfactory, at the time it happened and for a month afterwards; and yet he had the assurance to say in his minute: " As the Dhar Durbar had in its service Konkanee and " other Sepoys distinct from Affghans and Mukranees, " it never was explained to my satisfaction (indeed, no

---

* Parliamentary Paper, No. 200, of 1859, page 10.

† Parliamentary Paper, No. 30, of 1861, page 32; para. 6, and page 37, annexure 2.

" explanation was ever attempted), how a strong fort
" containing the treasure of the State, and easily tenable
" by the Sepoys against the Affghans and Mukranees
" (the Mussulmen), could have passed into the hands of
" the latter without the connivance of the Durbar."*
Is it possible to conceive a more unblushing mis-statement? And yet this mis-statement was made the main charge against the Durbar, firstly, by Lord Canning's Government in 1858, and secondly, by the Home Government under Sir Charles Wood in 1860.

Before I leave this part of the subject, I must cite one more instance in which help was demanded by the Dhar Government. On the night of the 9th of October, the Mussulmen turned out in concert with all the rebels in the neighbourhood to make a combined attack on Bhopawur and Sirdapore. It transpired next morning that they had left only a weak party in the fort, and it occurred to the Ranee that the fort might be surprised during the expedition, though their destination was at first unknown. Accordingly she sent the news to Mhow, which was delivered on the following morning, October 11th,† and if the rebels had not returned the next day, October 12th, we might very likely have recaptured the fort without firing a shot, owing to this information, which would have been as much for our interest as the Ranee's (I mean our public interest—of course the overwhelming private interest of the Mhow column was prize-money).

Since all our information at that time was derived from the Durbar, I publish several of their communications in Appendix E, to show that at that time they

* Parliamentary Paper, No. 30, of 1861, page 19, para. 12.
† Parliamentary Paper, No. 200, of 1859, page 13.

were again complaining to the British authorities of the oppression of the rebels, and appealing to us to deliver them from it.

Nevertheless, on the 12th instant, Colonel Durand, on hearing of the outrages at Bhopawur and Sirdapore, at once wrote to Lord Canning, that: " Dhar must of " course be made responsible for the acts of the mer- " cenaries it chose to enlist but could not manage." * However slow to prevent the guilty, he was not slow to punish the innocent! but he had his reasons for being quick this time! On the 12th of October, after the destruction of two stations quite near him, he could not but see at length, and fear Lord Canning would see,† the fatal consequences of his " unaccountable " inaction;" therefore he hastened to throw the blame on the Dhar Government, lest some one else should throw it on him,—and Lord Canning fell into the snare.

The truth is, as I have shown the reader, that Colonel Durand's disorganisation of the Native Government, and long tolerance of its mutineers, made it more impossible for the Dhar State than for any other " to " control its mercenary troops."

---

* Parliamentary Paper, No. 200, of 1859, page 12.

† His Lordship's eyes do seem to have been opened for an instant, though only for an instant. When the report of the destruction of these stations first reached him, he inquired, " whether the force at " Mhow might not have acted against the insurgents ? " But between the question and the answer intervened all the operations against Dhar, the siege and capture of the fort, the decision formed on Col. Durand's recommendation to make the State responsible, &c., so that excuses for " unaccountable inaction," passed current easily when all was over.— *Vide* Mr. Edmonstone's letter of Nov. 4th, and Col. Durand's reply of Nov. 27th, in Parliamentary Paper, No. 200, of 1859, pages 14, 30.

CHAPTER V.

Action in India, on receiving Lord Stanley's orders to restore the Principality eventually to its young Rajah—Decision not to restore it.

THE first intimation of the decision of the Home Government in this case must have reached Lord Canning at latest in the beginning of July, 1858,* and the despatch formally announcing the orders of the Home Government reached him before the end of that month; Colonel Durand being then on special duty with him at Allahabad. After a few weeks' consideration, the Governor-General made up his mind to set Lord Stanley at defiance, and flatly disobey his orders; and on the 12th of August, 1858, Mr. Edmonstone, Secretary to the Government of India, was directed by him to write as follows to Sir Robert Hamilton, who had then resumed charge at Indore: "The Right Honorable the " Governor-General sees no reason whatever to alter or " modify the orders conveyed to you on the 8th of " February last, regarding the disposal of the treasure " and other property found in the fort of Dhar; nor " can his Lordship perceive any reasonable grounds for " questioning the justice of the decision conveyed in my " letter dated 7th of December, 1857, as to the seques-" tration of the Dhar State. You are requested, there-

* By a mail of about the same date as Lord Stanley's announcement in the House of Commons.

" fore, no longer to delay the announcement which you
" have been directed to make." *

The announcement was that the recommendation of Colonel Durand on the 14th of December, 1857, had been sanctioned by the Governor-General, in Mr. Beadon's letter of February 8th, 1858,† to the effect that, "as a reward to the troops engaged, and as a " politic example, the treasure, guns, &c., taken in " the Fort of Dhar, be granted as prize to the column " then serving before the place." The decision conveyed in Mr. Edmonstone's letter of December 7th, 1857, was that the Governor-General's agent should "explain to " the young chief (of Dhar) that while the Government " reserves to itself the right to dispose of the State " hereafter in such manner as may seem fitting, he can " never hope that it will be restored to him."‡

But the Governor-General seems not only to have made up his mind to set Lord Stanley's decision on the Dhar case at defiance, but to prevent his interfering again, by never letting him know what had been done in the matter. I ascertained by continual enquiry at the India Office, that all the private questions on the subject of the Secretary of State for India, and even a public despatch to the same effect, in March, 1859,§ not only failed to obtain any information, but even to receive a syllable of notice, until I got Mr. Bright to take up the matter in Parliament; and Mr. Edmonstone's letter, quoted above, was never divulged till nearly three years afterwards, in the session of 1861,

---

* Parliamentary Paper, No. 30, of 1861, page 31, para. 31.
† Parliamentary Paper, No. 200, of 1859, page 31.
‡ Parliamentary Paper, No. 200, of 1859, page 28, para. 3.
§ Parliamentary Paper, No. 200, of 1859, page 6.

when, from the supposed settlement of the question, and satisfaction given to Lord Stanley the session before, nobody was likely to read a Blue-book on the subject, and I believe nobody in this country did read it at the time.

With the help of this Blue-book I will now describe the events in India which led to Mr. Bright's interference.

It appears that about the time when Lord Stanley had this case under consideration at home, Sir Robert Hamilton, who had resumed his duties as Resident in the winter of 1857-58, was led to doubt the justice of the measures of the Government in India. I conjecture that he had heard comparatively little of the matter until after the sequestration of Dhar, on the 14th of February, 1858, as up to that time the Ranee and her friends never doubted that as soon as we had leisure we should make a stringent enquiry into the conduct of those members of the Durbar who had been arrested on suspicion, and that everything would then be satisfactorily explained and arranged. Not a Native in Malwa had any reason to apprehend that we should dethrone the young Rajah; and therefore I conjecture that they did not trouble Sir Robert Hamilton much about it at first, knowing how busy he was, and believing that all would come right in the end, while in the meantime the administration was going on smoothly under Captain Hutchinson. After the confiscation, on the contrary, I believe that Sir Robert Hamilton was inundated with appeals for justice, and fresh information, on the subject, for months together.

The first effect of this was that on the 5th of July, 1858, he addressed to the Government of India what he called a "reference," and the angry Government called a "remonstrance," on the aforesaid order of February 8th, to treat the Dhar treasure as prize-money. There was not a word in this "reference" that conveyed a personal reflection on Colonel Durand, or justified the violent and abusive style of his reply to it. Sir Robert observed simply that "the State of "Dhar had always been faithful and friendly;" that the mutinies had occurred just when its government was in the difficulties of a minority; that these difficulties had been increased by our turning loose into Malwa the mercenaries (Mussulmen) we removed from the Nizam's country, at the end of 1856, against which he had protested at the time; that a number of these mercenaries, being engaged by the factions who contended for power in Dhar during the minority, to strengthen themselves against each other, had seen their strength, combined, and seized the fort; that our troops were marched to Dhar to dislodge them, without any declaration of war against the State, and as it was believed, to support the minor we had put on the throne; that the Dhar officials furnished us with supplies, the minor Rajah was received in Durbar by the Acting Agent during the siege, and treated with every consideration, and nothing passed to indicate that we considered the State in rebellion, and looked upon the minor Rajah and his Government as enemies; that when a breach was made, the fort was evacuated, and we took possession; but under these circumstances, and "in the absence of any declaration of war," he hoped the Government would re-consider its decision to treat the Dhar treasure as prize-money.*

* Parliamentary Paper, No. 30, of 1861, pages 15, 16.

Unfortunately, Lord Canning was committed to a despotic course, and already knew that Lord Stanley was committed to its reversal; his pride forbade him to retract, and he handed over Sir Robert Hamilton's "reference" to Colonel Durand, undoubtedly intending him to treat the old Resident as "disaffected," and to give no quarter to the "remonstrance."*

On this Colonel Durand wrote his Minute of July 22nd, 1858,† in which he endeavours to vindicate all the unjust measures towards the State of Dhar, which Lord Canning had been induced to sanction at his recommendation.

The first thing I must notice in this Minute is, that, although Colonel Durand does not scruple to charge Sir Robert Hamilton with "suppression, distortion, and "evasion of important facts,"‡ I have already convicted Colonel Durand himself of suppressing and evading the two most important facts in the whole case! viz.—

1st. His break up of the Regency, and complete disorganisation of the Government by cancelling the Minister's appointment; which I have proved by the production of two documents, probably never seen by Sir Robert Hamilton, certainly now published for the first time.

2nd. The mutiny of the 31st of August, when the rebels seized the fort, and held it until we marched to dislodge them, and when he refused the timely assistance demanded by the Native State.

---

* Parliamentary Paper, No. 30, of 1861, page 16.

† Parliamentary Paper, No. 30, of 1861, pages 17 to 27. As this Minute must henceforward be often referred to, I shall confine such references to its paragraphs.

‡ Para. 41 of Col. Durand's Minute.

With regard to the first of these facts, Colonel Durand distinctly states at para. 4 of his Minute, and confidently assumes throughout, that, "the administration of the State was in as uninterrupted and undisturbed action after as it had been before the death of the late Rajah:" he knowing better than almost any man alive how untrue such a statement was! (Lord Canning little understood the man he trusted to!)

With regard to the second fact, he states at paras. 14, 15, of his Minute, that the "first burst" of the insurrection was the outbreak at Dhar on "*the 10th of October*," thus utterly ignoring the outbreak and seizure of the fort by the Mussulman portion of the troops on the 31st of August; and suppressing the forty intervening days, during which the Native Government had been at their mercy, and had been compelled to take into its pay about as many more of their so-called "brethren and relations," some of those "parties" mentioned by Colonel Durand,* who had been driven from the west by an advance of Bombay troops in that quarter (which advance was made, by the way, in the end of August and beginning of September: for there was no "unaccountable inaction" anywhere but at Mhow!)

However, I will now examine in detail those portions of Colonel Durand's Minute which attempt to prove more against the Dhar Government than "inability to control its mercenary troops;" and I think the substance of them may be resolved into the following specific charges:—

1st. That the government had treacherously levied

---

* Page 19, para. 10.

hostile mercenary troops even before 1st of July* (date of the Indore mutiny).

2nd. That the government had connived at the seizure of the fort by those troops.†

3rd. That the government "began the war" ‡ by various direct or indirect acts of hostility: to wit, by marching its troops to Bhopawur, Sirdapore, and Gbojree on the Bombay road, and attacking and burning the said places; by repulsing our cavalry at Nalcha, and forcing Major Robertson "to open the "campaign by clearing the Bombay road, and covering "Mundlaisir from insult;" by welcoming the rebels on their return from Sirdapore, giving their leader a dress of honour, and receiving part of the booty at the palace;§ by arraying all its troops against us when our column reached the fort, because several Mahratta horsemen were killed in action under the walls; ‖ by deceiving Captain Hutchinson through its Vakeel in the middle of October, as to its negotiations with the mutinous mercenaries, and the numbers it had enlisted; ¶ by communicating with the Shahzada at Mundesor, and treating his emissaries with the greatest attention and civility;** and finally by sending its elephants for ammunition during the siege.††

4th. That the government was "clearly demon-"strated" to have the garrison under its orders, because letters from the garrison to the Shahzada asking for relief were intercepted during the siege, and because when the garrison showed a white flag they asked to

---

* Para. 9.   † Para. 12.   ‡ Paras. 34, 35, 15, 18, 21.
§ Paras. 17, 15; 35.   ‖ Para. 25.
¶ Para. 17.   ** Paras. 17, 35.   †† Para. 31.

speak to Captain Hutchinson in the presence of some one of the Durbar.*

These are the various counts of Colonel Durand's indictment against the Dhar Government, and I will now answer them in detail, as they were assumed to be true by Lord Canning, in Mr. Edmonstone's despatch of August 12th, 1858, and again by Sir Charles Wood, in his despatch of February 14th, 1860, although *they had all been answered before Colonel Durand's Minute was written*, and were again satisfactorily answered by Sir Robert Hamilton's second despatch of August 30th, 1858.

1st.- With regard to the original entertainment of these troops "contrary to repeated orders?" The late Rajah had engaged every man of these troops who was in the service of the Dhar Government before the 1st of July; and Colonel Durand had stated on May 28th, 1857,† that the late Rajah "so administered his affairs " as to secure the esteem, the respect of the people and " chiefs of Western Malwa, as well as the approbation " of successive Residents and agents." The first entertainment of these troops was, therefore, certainly not an act of treachery, and with regard to our "repeated orders" about them, it *was* true, as asserted by Sir Robert Hamilton on the 5th of July, and repeated by him, in spite of Colonel Durand's contradiction, on the 30th of August, 1858, that our expulsion of hordes of these mercenaries from the Nizam's dominions at the end of 1856, did create a serious difficulty for the Malwa States, in all of which, particularly in Gwalior and Bhopal, their friends contrived to get many of them

---

* Para. 33; see also page 35, paras. 32, 33.

† Parliamentary Paper, No. 200, of 1859, page 8.

enlisted, because they had "got a hold," as Sir Robert Hamilton observes, which he explains by adding that "their jemadars were generally creditors of the State." The fact is, that many of these Arabs, who are, as a rule, orderly enough when regularly paid, are among the most notorious *usurers* of India; they seem to live for money making; and consequently, with the loose financial system of Native Courts, they generally get a pecuniary hold on the government, wherever they have been settled for some time, which makes it difficult to dismiss their levies, and almost impossible to do so all at once. The thing would have been done in time, in obedience to our orders, throughout Malwa; but Dhar was no more responsible for not doing it off hand, than Scindiah was, or any other of our allies. The Bhegum of Bhopal employed more of these Mussulmen than any one else, and yet she has since been rewarded for her fidelity by the large jaghire of Bhairseah cut off the Dhar State, and formerly contributing £10,000 a-year, or one-fifth of its income. After all, the number of these Dhar mercenaries, either on the 1st of July or the 31st of August, was not very formidable to a moveable column containing, besides the Native troops, some hundreds of British infantry and cavalry! The Dhar Mussulman force numbered 210 men at the late Rajah's death, and was not increased until after the Court mourning was over in July. New levies of 129 men were made in August, owing to the intrigues I have described, raising the total of Mukranees, Vellaitees, Pathans, and Arabs to 339 men, at the time they seized the fort. During the next forty days they forced the Government to enlist 258 more "brethren and relations," raising the total to about

600 men in the middle of October. But at that time, besides these troops, there were hordes of armed rebels in the fort, in the town, and encamped about it, and these forces, beyond even the nominal control of the Dhar Government, together with its own mutineers, so oppressed both the Government and the people, that the Durbar again began to entreat us to deliver it from their oppression, in letters which I have already referred to; and as the advance of our column took place a week after these fresh entreaties were made, it was supposed " throughout Malwa," as Sir Robert Hamilton observed,* that our advance was made in consequence of these entreaties. Colonel Durand admits the presence of hostile independent forces, not even nominally under the control of the Dhar Government, in one of his charges against the Durbar, on the 30th of October, the last day but one of the siege, when he says: "a portion " of their (Dhar) troops, are a part of the garrison now " holding out against us."†

2nd. I have already fully answered and disproved the charge of connivance in the seizure of the fort; so I need not repeat what I have said.

3rd. There are so many acts by which the Dhar Government is said to have " begun a war," that I must take them separately.

1st. Out of the four places named as the scene of active hostility on the part of the Durbar, Bhopawur and Sirdapore are the only two where any Dhar troops went. Goojree was burnt by some Bheels, who were tried, convicted, and hung for it, in March, 1858.‡

---

* Parliamentary Paper, No. 30, of 1861, page 33, para. 13.
† Parliamentary Paper, No. 200, of 1859, page 18, para. 3.
‡ Parliamentary Paper, No. 30, of 1861, page 34, para. 22.

With regard to Nalcha, the report cited by Colonel Durand, of "the Native cavalry officer commanding "the detachment," was proved to be a lie, within a few days after it was made. On first hearing of this "repulse at Nalcha," Colonel Durand was "very angry" (as usual), and threatened, in the presence of several witnesses, to make the Durbar responsible for this act of hostility. But luckily he ordered an immediate inquiry, which elicited the following facts: When the cavalry detachment reached Nalcha, where the "troops " so hostile and strong" amounted to ten local horsemen and twenty police!—when the cavalry reached Nalcha, the authorities offered them every kind of provision they required; but happening to hear in conversation, from a Mussulman of the place, one of the countless rumours prevalent in those days, that the Dhar mutineers were threatening an advance in that direction, the Native officer took the alarm and returned to Mhow with his detachment, without so much as having seen an enemy! Major Keating, who conducted this inquiry, at once communicated the result to the authorities at Mhow, and moreover at once discharged the head-man of Nalcha, who had been placed in arrest, and no more was heard of the matter again until Colonel Durand revived it in his Minute. By the way, he adds in his Minute that, the "cavalry sent out to "reconnoitre towards Nalcha" were "witness to the "burning of Goojree bungalow." This graphic but superfluous detail is characteristic of his style, which always aims at giving the "colour locale." What a painting those few words suggest: they "were witness "to the burning!" We see the picturesque groups of the Hyderabad contingent, stopping (of course before their repulse at Nalcha, they would not be inclined to stop afterwards)—stopping on an Indian ghaut, in the grey of the morning, while their gallant leader points with his sword,

"And careless eyes the blood that dims it's shine."

It is a pretty picture! but I must spoil it; for how could the cavalry see Goojree bungalow, through physical obstacles, over fifteen miles across country? and, worse still, how could they see over four days of time? since it is certain that they returned and reported on the 12th of October; and it was proved in a court of justice that Goojree was not burnt till the 16th. I presume that Colonel Durand had forgotten the true date of this event; and, finding in the papers he referred to, a rumour of it (in a report of Captain Hutchinson's) four days before it actually happened, he at once imagined this stage effect for the cavalry, to make them "witness" it. At the same time, though I can imagine a man's forgetting the exact date of burning a house, which was too common a thing unfortunately in those days, I certainly cannot understand Colonel Durand's forgetting the history of the "repulse at Nalcha," because it was the explosion of this impudent fable of the "hos-"tile and strong troops" at Nalcha which enabled the Mhow force to march on Dhar, as it did, eight days afterwards, in two separate columns, which were about twelve miles apart when they passed north and south of Nalcha.

With regard to Major Robertson's "opening the cam-"paign by clearing the Bombay road, and covering "Mundlaisir from insult," both the "clearance" and the "insult" are quite imaginary! Major Robertson soon found that not a man from Dhar had come in that direction, and he did not go below the Ghauts. In fact, in spite of all the rumours of those days, the Dhar rebels never ventured to move south, within reach of a British column. The utmost they dared was to wait for the column under the guns of the fort; and even then it was, as they wrote to the Shahzada, "not of " our own free will, but at your request, and with the assurance of your support." *

With regard to the attack on Bhopawur and Sirdapore, there is no evidence that the Dhar Government was in any way responsible for the concurrence of its mutineers in this outrage, while there is abundant evidence that the Government was quite innocent of their deeds, and powerless to restrain their passions, including the evidence of Colonel Durand himself, which I must again quote here. When the Dhar troops mutinied on August 31st, Colonel Durand endorsed a similar opinion from Captain Hutchinson, with the words, the Dhar Government is "impotent to control " its levies."† During September he has recorded that the number of these levies was "rapidly increased by " the advent of parties of from twenty to forty from " the side of Dohud and the west,"‡ which must have made the Dhar Government still more "impotent to " control them." (These parties were driven into Dhar by our advance from Guzerat). On the 12th of October, *after* the attack on Bhopawur and Sirdapore, he repeated that the Dhar Government " could not manage

---

* *Vide* Parliamentary Paper, No. 200, of 1859, page 23, annexure No. 2.

† Parliamentary Paper, No. 200, of 1859, page 10.

‡ Parliamentary Paper, No. 30, of 1861, page 19, para. 10.

"its mercenaries."* Such was the uniform tenor of his evidence until the outrages which had resulted from his "unaccountable inaction" made it his interest to throw the blame on the Dhar Government, to shift it from his own shoulders. Then he changed his tone. He turned quite round, and contradicted his former reports, arguing that, so far from not being "able to manage its mercenaries," the Dhar Durbar "plunged unprovoked into hostilities with the British Government," and "began a war," and "took the initiative," and "struck the first blow," by this attack on two of our stations. And it is on the wholly unsupported witness of this man—witness stamped on the face of it with such self-contradiction—that our Government assumed the truth of his incredible charge, that the weak, divided Régency of a puny Native State boldly "began a war" against the mighty power of our empire, in the flowing tide of our success! For be it remembered, that a complete revolution had occurred in our prospects by the 10th of October; and every educated man in India knew then, that the triumph of the British Government was absolutely certain. Many events had contributed to this; the fall of Delhi a month before, and our successes in various quarters since then; the arrival of Sir Colin Campbell, and announcement of unlimited reinforcements from England; the arrival of the China troops; and the confirmed adhesion to us of the Native princes, including Holkar, the powerful neighbour, and, of course, the pattern of the Dhar Ranee. For at that time the younger Ranee was fast sinking, and the elder Ranee was chiefly responsible for the administration, though

* Parliamentary Paper, No. 200, of 1859, page 12.

her brother, and the minister, and others took part in it, not one of them being the recognised head of the Durbar, which ought to have been the case, and would have been if Colonel Durand had done his duty. But to return to his charge. It is on record that, before the mutiny of its troops, the Dhar Government rendered us all the assistance it possibly could, and that, after their mutiny, it appealed to us for help to control them, until not merely refused but silenced by our officers. It is on record that it sent us all the intelligence it could of the rebels' movements, and that after their return from Bhopawur and Sirdapore, when they turned the guns of the fort on the town, repeatedly threatened to sack it, and used to come and take what they wanted without paying, besides many other outrages, the Dhar Government began again to appeal to our authorities for help, as if its only hope was in the British column. It is on record that when at last our " unaccountable inaction " ceased, and the Mhow force marched against the rebels, the Dhar Government used all the administrative power left it, in giving us help, and procuring us supplies; and that, when we had made no progress in the siege, it informed us where there was a weak part in the fort, which could easily be breached, and sent us persons acquainted with the locality, and plans of the works, which ensured the success of our operations within a few days of our receiving the information—a success the more valuable as it was obtained without loss to the column. And with all these proofs on record of "its inability to con-" trol its troops," and of its fidelity and good service to us, and reliance on us both before and after the 10th of October—and there is no other conceivable proof of fidelity that it could have given—surely it is as revolting to common sense to assert that the Dhar Government wilfully "began a war" with us, by the attack of its mutineers on Bhopawur and Sirdapore, as it would be to say that the British Government "began a "war" with itself, when its own mutineers plundered and burnt so many other stations!

With regard to the charge of " welcoming the rebels " on their return from Sirdapore, giving their leader " a dress of honor, and receiving part of the booty " at the palace." First, the "part of the booty" consisted of two three-pounder guns, which the rebels, who did what they liked, brought from Sirdapore, and planted outside the palace, and afterwards could not take away with them, because those who got into the fort again after their defeat on the arrival of our column, were too much hurried, and the majority fled at once to Burnugger. Second, the negotiation with the rebels on their return from Sirdapore, is thus explained by Sir Robert Hamilton: "When Bheem Rao came before " me in December, an enquiry being commenced by " me, he did not deny that he met the returning " Vellaitees, but stated that he was sent with the object " to induce them to encamp outside the town, and to " prevent them coming into it to plunder it, as was " reported to be their intention; his statement is an-" nexed, and I am bound to add, it is supported by " what I have heard from others."* This is a sufficient answer to the above charge, but I must also add that Bheem Rao (the Ranee's brother) was afterwards released on giving security for £200 (a tacit admission of his innocence!), and that the whole authority for this

* Parliamentary Paper, No. 30, of 1861, page 33, para. 14.

alleged treachery in the Dhar Government, the whole authority from first to last was a report of fugitives from *Bhopawur!* who *said it was* a topic of conversation in Dhar!"* Now, even in Europe, where the press has so much power, the views of kings and cabinets are not certainly known to the public, though they have through the press, a means of contradicting unfounded rumours about them; but in the Native States of India, where, for want of a press, there is still less chance of the views of princes and cabinets being certainly known, and where, for want of a press, there is no means of contradicting unfounded rumours about them, it does seem monstrous to condemn and confiscate a State, and punish its royal family with the utmost severity, on the strength of mere rumours among fugitives from *another* State! rumours opposed to the uniform language and action of the foreign State inculpated by them! Certainly if we are to act in future on these principles in India, if the fate of Native States is to hang upon what may be *said to be* a "topic of conversation" in them, by strangers who dwell in another territory, there is no Native State in India that is not in danger of confiscation, no princely family that may not anticipate the undeserved punishment which fell on the house of Puar.

I come now to the charge that the Government had arrayed the whole of its troops against us on the day we reached the fort, because several Mahratta horsemen were among the slain.

I have already stated that, after confiscating the state, we retained a hundred of its Sepoys, the Konkanees

---

* Parliamentary Paper, No. 30, of 1861, page 20, and Parliamentary Paper, No. 200, of 1859, No. 317, dated Oct. 15th, 1857.

and Bundelas, in our service, because they had never mutinied when in the service of the Native Government, and had never been arrayed against us; and I added that these troops were employed by the Native State as palace, city, and treasure guards, because they were more trusted than the Mussulmen, or Poorbeah Sepoys. Colonel Durand admits, in para. 26, that on the same day that the action took place, we found the Rajah in his palace in the city, with a guard of these Sepoys (Konkanees and Bundelas) about him, and he admits, at para. 33, that after the evacuation of the fort we found the treasure guard, of Konkanees and Bundelas, still in it, who made no opposition, but showed us where the treasure was kept. It is therefore certain that "the " whole of the Durbar troops " were *not* " drawn out in " position against us " on the 22nd of October;[*] but the deaths of several non-combatants on that day, were reported to the Dhar Government to have happened in this way. When the column reached the fort, the garrison turned out, and took up a position under the guns of the fort, with all the armed rabble in the neighbourhood, to fight us in the field. On this, most of the citizens, and among them from 20 to 30 sowars, went out to see the fight. These people, with the exception of the sowars, were unarmed; the sowars were armed because it is the custom in the East for a soldier never to leave his house without his weapons, but they all went merely to look on, without any intention of interfering, or getting into danger themselves; nevertheless, they did get into danger, and two or three of them were killed by musket balls. Such was the report made to the Government, which could not have foreseen

[*] As stated by Col. Durand, in para. 25.

this impulse of curiosity, and could not have prevented the indulgence of it by any orders on a day of such excitement and confusion.

With regard to the charge of " deceiving Captain Hut-" chinson through its Vakeel in the middle of October, " as to its negotiations with the mutinous mercenaries, " and the numbers it had enlisted?" I have already given Sir Robert Hamilton's explanation of the negotiations referred to, and there never was any intended variation from the representation made by the Ranee in her letter to the Governor-General, as to the number of troops in the service of the State. The Ranee stated the number at 600 Mussulmen (and I shall hereafter show that some of these Mussulmen tried repeatedly to negotiate, and declared that our refusal to hear them forced them into the rebel ranks), exclusive of about 200 others, of whom one-half were so clear from any suspicion of mutiny, that we kept them in our service. There may have been a mistake of the Vakeel's, by giving a statement of "new" levies as "new and old " levies," on the 10th of October, but it is certain that there was no intention to understate their numbers, because on the 12th the Vakeel informed Captain Hutchinson, in one of the letters cited by me, speaking of all the mercenaries who had returned from Sirdapore, whether mutineers or rebels, "it is rumoured that the " Budmashes are 1,500 in number." This and other intelligence was sent when it was difficult and dangerous to send communications, for the rebels tried to intercept them.

With regard to the charge of "communicating with " the Shahzada, and treating his emissaries with the " greatest attention and civility?" the only authorities were the aforesaid "fugitives from Bhopawur," and a previous communication from the Dhar Government itself.*

The last charge of "sending its elephants for ammu-"nition during the siege," was not merely equally groundless, it was a transparent excuse for one of those wanton acts of plunder that abounded in those days—an act against which the Dhar Government protested at once emphatically, both verbally and by letter. The truth of the story was this: Five or six elephants were sent out as usual—they go almost every day—to fetch their forage, grass, or branches of trees from the jungles, and the drivers had no weapons with them except the axes and scythes necessary to cut forage, when, the instant they left the city, not the fort, they were pursued and captured by a picquet of the Hyderabad contingent, always eager for "loot." There was not an armed man with these elephants; in fact, no enemies could then leave the fort, or get into it, on account of our picquets; two individuals who did escape from it into the town were made over to us; and at that very time the Durbar were securing and damping with water all the powder in the city shops, and restoring to our officers all the shot and shell that came from the fort, in obedience to an order from Captain Hutchinson, which I print in the appendix.† This incident accidentally furnishes another striking proof of the innocence of the Dhar Government by showing that they had not prepared the fort in any way for a siege; they had not mounted twelve out of eighteen heavy guns that were in the fort, and they had not

---

* Parliamentary Paper, No. 200, of 1859, pages 13, 14.
† *Vide* Appendix G.

provided ammunition, so that when the fort was evacuated, and Colonel Durand was anxious and impatient to have it blown up,* he actually could not get it done for want of powder! To return to the elephants: Colonel Durand admits in his Minute† that "the elephants were claimed by the State as soon as they were known to have fallen into our hands;" but adds in the next paragraph, "that as the com-
"missiarat required elephants, they were sold to that
"department at a reasonable valuation, and the proceeds
"divided among the captors by the military authorities,
"as an encouragement to the Nizam's cavalry." Ah! there was plenty of such *encouragement* in those days: the passion for "loot" was indulged at that time to an excess that would be incredible to home readers.

I now come to the last count of his indictment, viz., that the Dhar Government was "clearly demonstrated" to have the garrison under its orders, by intercepted letters from the garrison to the Shahzada during the siege, and by a demand from the garrison when they showed a white flag, to speak to Captain Hutchinson in the presence of some one of the Durbar, which Colonel Durand refused to permit.

No doubt this charge may be a sufficiently "clear
"demonstration" of the guilt of a Native State, when we have a mind to annex it, because any falsehood or absurdity is reason enough, when the wolf has made up his mind to devour the lamb; but for any other purpose the charge is so preposterous, that I really feel degraded by the necessity of answering it. Let any one look at the letters again, which are printed in the

---

* Parliamentary Paper, No. 200, of 1859, page 22.

† Parliamentary Paper, No. 30, of 1861, page 23, paras. 31, 32.

first Dhar Blue-book,* how on earth could these letters
"clearly demonstrate" that the writers were under the
orders of the Dhar Government? if they proved anything, it was the very reverse; that the writers were
not under the orders of the Dhar Government, but of
the Shahzada, as I have no doubt they were.* Moreover, these letters, which are employed to prove that
the Government communicated with the Shahzada
through the garrison, these intercepted letters were not
from the garrison at all, but from the rebels at Burnugger! so easy is it for the wolf to "clearly demon-
"strate" the necessity of eating the lamb! Again,
how could the demand of the garrison to speak to
Captain Hutchinson in the presence of some member of
the Durbar, prove anything against the Dhar Government, without hearing what they had to say? Over-
tures were repeatedly made by the garrison, according
to Colonel Durand, both before our column reached the
fort, and during the siege,† and on this occasion the
object of those who showed the white flag was explained
by Sir Robert Hamilton‡ to this effect, that, it was
known to the Durbar that there were separate parties
of Mussulman troops in the fort, and some of these
wished to obtain terms, on the plea that they had not
joined in the attack on Bhopawur and Sirdapore, and
had not committed themselves against the British
Government. If, as Colonel Durand asserts,§ the siege

---

* Parliamentary Paper, No. 200, of 1859, page 23.

† Parliamentary Paper, No. 200, of 1859, page 17, and Parliamentary Paper, No. 30, of 1861, page 22, para. 24.

‡ Parliamentary Paper, No. 30, of 1861, pages 35, 36.

§ Parliamentary Paper, No. 30, of 1861, page 26, para. 44, and
Parliamentary Paper, No. 200, of 1861, page 18, para. 7.

was " a most critical operation," and "time was pre-
" cious " on the day the garrison showed the white flag,
he should at least have heard their proposals before he
refused to allow them to capitulate; but he says, "he
" directed Captain Hutchinson to return with orders to
" open fire, which was immediately done."* Instead of
listening to offers of capitulation, he preferred to storm
what he calls "a difficult breach."† He says that,
" from the form of the ramparts right and left, and the
" facility of defending the head of the breach, he was
" surprised that Affghans should have shrunk from its
" defence," and that "a storm costly in life and thereby
" paralysing the column, might have produced results
" exceedingly difficult to estimate." In spite of its
exceeding difficulty, he estimates these "results" in the
next sentence, as follows:—1st. The handing over "not
" only Malwa but also Rajpootana" as a prey to the
Shahzada (and his "rabble"). 2nd. Another mutiny
of Holkar's troops at Indore. 3rd. Setting Eastern
Malwa in flames, treading down the Regent of Bhopal,
and subverting that State from a friendly to a hostile
one. 4th. Not freeing the line of the Nerbudda, and
rolling back insurrection so as to keep the south of
India clear. . . . Why did he not add, setting the
seas on fire? surely such ridiculous exaggeration, such
puffing of the importance of his own operations, is
quite unworthy of a British soldier. I have shown
how he had himself paralysed the column for nearly
three months at Mhow; and what mischief it had done,
by encouraging the gathering of an armed rabble in the
neighbourhood, and permitting anarchy, rioting, and

* Parliamentary Paper, No. 200, of 1861, page 18, para. 4.
† Parliamentary Paper, No. 30, of 1861, page 26.

outrages at Dhar, Bhopawur, and Sirdapore. But I have also shown that the mischiefs caused by his " un-" accountable inaction," were rendered purely local, and comparatively harmless, by our vigorous action at the time in other parts of India.

Having thus answered every count of his indictment against the Dhar Government, I must say a few words on some other points in his minute, to show that he completely failed to refute Sir Robert Hamilton's objections to appropriating the Dhar treasures as prize-money.

Sir Robert had stated that our troops were marched to Dhar at the request of the Native Government, to dislodge the mutineers and rebels from its fort and territory, and, as was believed, to support the minor we had put on the throne; that the Dhar officials furnished us with supplies, &c., and the minor Rajah was received by the acting agent during the siege and treated with every consideration, and nothing passed to indicate that we looked upon the minor Rajah and the Dhar Government as enemies; and, therefore, when the fort was evacuated, we were not justified in appropriating the Dhar treasure as prize-money, *without any declaration of war.*

Colonel Durand rests his reply to this on three several grounds. 1st. That no one could have understood that the advance of our column was to support the minor we had put on the throne; not any of the States under the Central Agency, because their Vakeels had been told the contrary; and he was "at a loss to " conceive who would have looked upon the movement " of our troops in the light set forth by Sir Robert " Hamilton." 2nd. That though the minor Rajah was received in Durbar during the siege, what passed did indicate that we should treat him and his government as enemies. 3rd. That although there was no necessity for a declaration of war, because the Dhar Government "began a war" with us, that his dismissal of one of the Dhar Vakeels amounted to a declaration of war.

To take these in order, 1st. As Colonel Durand is at at a loss to conceive who could have looked upon the advance of our troops as meant to support the Dhar Government, I will mention two or three parties who must have done so:—

1st. In the communications from the Dhar Government which preceded the advance of our troops, I find the following phrases: "The Budmashes are increasing "day by day, and therefore you will be kind enough "in making arrangements for their punishment, and "restoring the tranquility of the State, as it looks to "you for assistance." Again: "The Durbar looks to "you as its well-wisher and supporter, and hopes that "you will render any assistance in your power at this "critical time. You will not fail to show that kindness "at this time which you showed heretofore." Again: "The only confidence of the Rajah now is in you, "and you should make the best arrangement in your "judgment."*

2nd. In the communication from Captain Hutchinson to the Dhar Government, already referred to,† on the first day of the siege, October 23rd, his letter begins (after compliments) with these words: "The "Durbar professes to be in friendly relations with the "British Government, and on account of this the Offg.

---

* See Appendix F.   † See Appendix G.

"Agent to Govr. Genl. (Colonel Durand), with a
"column, had come to assist them. . . . ." There is a
curious thing! Colonel Durand is "at a loss to con-
"ceive" who could have supposed that the advance of
our column was meant to assist the Dhar Government,
and yet his own confidential agent, writing by his
orders, on the first day of the siege, says in so many
words, that the "column had come to assist them."

3rd. In the communication from the Ranees to
Colonel Durand on October the 31st, the last day of
the siege, after remarking that all had gone on well
until the mutiny of their Mussulman troops "carried
"matters to the present pitch," they continue: "We
"have every hope of safety notwithstanding, from a
"patron, well-wisher, and supporter of friends, like
"you. You have been put to great trouble in punish-
"ing the rebels, and in marching to this with troops.
"We shall never forget this obligation; the honour of
"the State rests with you. The support (nigahs) of
"the Company's Government kept up 'bundobust' up
"to this time, and we had no trouble. These 'Bud-
"mashes' have now given us much annoyance, and
"your coming to punish them has caused us much
"satisfaction. To save the town, the rayts, and the
"treasure in the fort, rests with you at the present
"juncture, and we are satisfied that, whatever you do
"will promote the good of the people and the State."*
So *they* also understand that, in Captain Hutchinson's
phrase, the column "had come to assist them;" and
Colonel Durand said not a word to undeceive them.†

---

* Parliamentary Paper, No. 30 of 1861, page 41.

† See Sir R. Hamilton's remarks on this, Parliamentary Paper, No. 30, of 1861, page 36, par. 34.

Finally I deny that any of the Vakeels of the Central Agency had been told that the movement of our troops was an act of war against the Dhar Government, and I deny that any of them looked upon it in that light. It would be quite easy to examine the Vakeels now on this point.

2nd. Colonel Durand's misrepresentations as to his treating the Rajah "like a private gentleman, and not "like the ruler of the State," at the Durbar of October 26th, are so clearly and authoritatively exposed by Sir Robert Hamilton in his minute of August 30th, 1858,* that it is scarcely necessary for me to add a word on the matter, but perhaps I ought to glance at a minor misrepresentation which Sir Robert passed over. Colonel Durand says, para. 27, that during the siege he received many messages from the Ranee, "who was "anxious then to adopt the line now taken in favor of "the State by Sir Robert Hamilton;" that "his replies "admitted of no misconstruction," but that, "to put "the matter beyond cavil, he requested the attendance "of the minor Rajah, the minister, &c., at a public "Durbar," thus implying that he *took the initiative* in procuring this interview, which was not the case.

I have already shown that the interpretation of our movement by the Ranees was the same as that of Captain Hutchinson; and Sir Robert Hamilton has shown that nothing occurred at the Durbar to alter that interpretation, in spite of Colonel Durand's bullying the unfortunate minister, who has had his innocence more completely proved by every subsequent inquiry. I will only add that the Dhar Government *took the initia-*

* Parliamentary Paper, No. 30, of 1861, pages 34, 35, paras. 27 to 31.

tive in procuring this interview between the Rajah and the agent, and the following translated extract from its vernacular diary gives the real origin of this public Durbar:—" The Durbar Vakeel was ordered to intimate " to the Agent Governor-General that since his arrival " he has not been to visit the Rajah, and it was cus- " tomary for him to do so on all occasions of his advent " at Dhar, and this being communicated to the Agent, " an interview was appointed."

3rd. I have now come to the most critical point of this question, of our right to claim the Dhar treasure as prize money? Colonel Durand says there was no necessity for a "declaration of war," for two reasons, 1st. Because the Dhar Government " began a war" with us, which assertion I have shown to be untrue; 2nd. Because his summary dismissal of the Dhar Vakeel, with a message to the Durbar that they would be responsible for all that had happened, or might happen, "*was a declaration of war.*" (It is worthy of remark that this was the same sort of message he sent to Holkar after the mutiny of his troops, and which drew upon him the reprimand from Lord Elphinstone.)

Now, I undertake to prove that he did not dismiss any Dhar Vakeel, although he uttered the above threat in his anger on the 12th of October, on hearing of the famous " repulse at Nalcha." Captain Hutchinson had told him that he suspected his own Vakeel, the Vakeel of the Bhopawur Agency, Raghonath Narain, in consequence of the rumours of fugitives from Bhopawur, on which Colonel Durand wrote to him—" You may " *either* keep *or* send away the Dhar Vakeel of this " Agency;" that is, the Vakeel of Colonel Durand's own office, Govind Vishvas Rao, a totally different person, about whom Captain Hutchinson had expressed no suspicion.* As the dismissal was left to Captain Hutchinson's option by the words of the above note, neither of the Vakeels were dismissed; and Sir Robert Hamilton has proved that Govind Rao continued to regularly attend Colonel Durand, and afterwards attended him, until our attachment of the State left him no one to represent. Sir Robert has proved this, not only by his own personal knowledge, and by an affidavit of Govind Rao, but by three letters of the Vakeel to Colonel Durand, during the siege, with Colonel Durand's signature to the orders upon them. I will only add one more proof, which is *a letter from Colonel Durand himself to the Vakeel*, several days after the siege.; and here it is, dated 6th November, 1857, addressed to Govind Vishvas Rao, and signed by Colonel Durand:—" The British troops will march to-" morrow from Dhar, and will halt at Teesgaon Pinjray " on the 7th, and on the 8th at Nowza Kanwan, vil-" lages of your territory; and you are therefore desired " to keep all sorts of supplies ready for the camp at the " two villages, and repair the road, so that the troops " may not find difficulties in their march." In the Vakeel's answer to Colonel Durand, of the same date, after describing the plundering and atrocities of the mutineers and rebels in the districts referred to, he concludes with these words:—" Owing to the oppression " of the Budmashes, the neighbouring villages are all " being depopulated, and therefore the Durbar is at a " loss to know how to make arrangements for supplies " to the British troops. However the Durbar looks to " you for your kind assistance in putting down these

* Parliamentary Paper, No. 30, of 1861, page 33, para. 15.

"Budmashes." (So *they* still thought, six days after the siege, that "the Officiating Agent to Governor-"General, with a column, had come to assist them," as Captain Hutchinson had told them).

Having thus, to the best of my power, carefully examined every fact and every argument used by Colonel Durand to justify the severe measures recommended by him, and adopted by the Government of India, towards the State of Dhar; and having discussed every detail in which suspicion could attach to its Government, I think I am fairly entitled to conclude, not merely that nothing has been proved, but that nothing can be proved, against the Dhar Government of 1857, except the admitted inability to control its mercenary troops; and that Lord Stanley's original decision on this case was the right one, that, "we " could not consistently punish Dhar or any other " weak State, for its inability to control its troops, " when it was patent to the whole world that the more " powerful States of Gwalior and Indore, and even the " British Government itself, were unable to control " theirs."

Unfortunately the Government of India both could, and did, set the above decision at defiance. In about a fortnight after the receipt of Colonel Durand's minute, on the 12th of August, 1858, the Governor-General ordered Mr. Edmonstone to write a despatch to Sir Robert Hamilton, adopting all Colonel Durand's assertions and inferences, and concluding with the orders I have already cited, to treat the Dhar treasure as prize-money, and to adhere to the confiscation of the State. In vain did Sir Robert Hamilton bravely submit further explanations to the Government, on the 30th of August, 1858, completely refuting the arguments addressed to him, and once more urging on Government that the Dhar treasure was "*not lawfully at its disposal;*" and that the restoration of the young Rajah "would " redound to the honor of our name, and be received " with deep gratitude as an earnest of our clemency, " and go far to allay the irritation and alarm which " have so widely spread throughout the country, owing " to the idea that our policy has aimed at getting rid " of every Native chief by any pretext, so as to absorb " and annex every territory held by a Native prince, " whether small or great."* It was all in vain. By Colonel Durand's advice Lord Canning had made up his mind to punish Dhar, and he inflicted the punishment.

* Parliamentary Paper, No. 30, of 1861, page 36, para. 36.

CHAPTER VI.

Notices of the Subject in the House of Commons—Second promise of the Home Government, under Sir Charles Wood, to restore Dhar to its Rajah, and evasion of this promise.

WHEN in June, 1858, I sent the joyful news to India that Lord Stanley had decided on the restoration of his Raj to the young prince of Dhar, believing that this trouble was happily over, I little thought that six years afterwards I should be fighting as hard a battle as ever to get this original decision carried into effect! Yet so it is. And, meanwhile, the man who sacrificed Dhar to save his own reputation, has had a career of uninterrupted prosperity, and nearly *carte blanche* to do as he liked with the Native Princes, either in the Cabinet of Lord Canning, or in the Council of Sir Charles Wood, or as Foreign Secretary for India. He has been placed where he could "feed fat the grudge he bore" to some of them. By the way, àpropos to the reason for sacrificing Dhar, I am sorry to say I have known many instances in which the faults or blunders of European officials in India have been visited on their Native officers, who were either perfectly innocent, or who had even protested against the conduct which gave offence to the Government. Yet the head Native officer has been deliberately sacrificed to save his English superior.

Long before the year 1858 was over, I was undeceived as to the finality of Lord Stanley's decision in the Dhar case. I found at home that the India office could get no notice whatever taken of its despatch; and in India, that the confiscation of the State was carried out so mercilessly that the privations and distress of the poor Ranee and her relatives and dependents were painful to think of. So matters went on till the Session of 1859, when the Home Government, goaded by continual enquiries, began to feel that Lord Canning's treatment of its decision was personally humiliating; so, as private letters could do nothing, in March, 1859, another formal despatch was sent on the subject of Dhar, and in April the papers in the case were given to the House of Commons, on the motion of Mr. J. B. Smith. Still not one word of answer could be obtained from India, where the sufferings of the royal family continued to increase; so, at the close of the Session, I asked Mr. Bright to notice the subject in the House, which he did in such emphatic language,* and with such pointed allusion to the insult offered to Lord Stanley by the Governor-General, that Sir Charles Wood, then Secretary of State for India, found it would be absolutely necessary to give satisfaction to Lord Stanley, and to English public opinion, in the ensuing Session.

Accordingly he at length obliged Lord Canning to reply, which he did, by entreating Sir Charles Wood to uphold the confiscation of Dhar, in his letter of December 6th, 1859.

But to openly affront Lord Stanley was more than

---

* See Hansard, 2nd vol. of 2nd Session of 1859, pages 811, 812.

Sir Charles Wood dared do, or than any English cabinet would have allowed him to do. Lord Stanley enjoyed great social and political advantages by the gift of fortune. Noble birth, immense wealth, a place next to the leader of the most powerful party in the State, all these things nature had given him, and he had doubled his natural advantages by his intelligent application to business, and particularly at the period in question, by his enlightened administration of Indian affairs. Everybody felt that his hardworking career at the India Office had commenced an era of progress in every department; everybody had hailed the proclamation which he advised the Queen to address to the princes and people of India, and his immediate action upon it by measures to stop the Inam resumptions, &c., as acts of the highest statesmanship; everybody instinctively felt, and I shall presently give some better reasons than instinct for this feeling, that the proclamation began " a " new policy" in India, which would make our empire more secure, and our rule in that country more creditable to us; finally, everybody had approved of his opposing the annexation system in the case of Dhar.

It was, therefore, imperative to satisfy Lord Stanley, whose honor was now at stake, and rather difficult at the same time to satisfy other parties; nevertheless, with Colonel Durand then at his elbow, Sir Charles Wood contrived a mode of doing it, as follows: he wrote a despatch, dated 14th of February, 1860,* destined to be kept secret until the whole affair had blown over, which began by justifying Lord Canning's policy, re-affirming the guilt of those members of the Dhar Go-

* Parliamentary Paper, No. 30; of 1861, pages 45, 46.

vernment who had been virtually acquitted in private a year before, after enquiries on the spot; especially condemning them for that seizure of the fort by the mutineers, which had been explained even to Colonel Durand's satisfaction at the time; in short, entirely reversing the language of the Home Government under Lord Stanley; then ordering, solely as a matter of expediency, the conditional restoration of the Raj to the young prince when he came of age; making the condition one by which the restoration could easily be prevented at that time; and meanwhile allowing Lord Canning to confiscate the district of Bhairseah, which contributed £10,000 a year, or one-fifth of the income of the State of Dhar (we had taken this district under our own management, for our own political purposes, and agreed to pay Dhar £10,000 a year on account of it, but under our management it had not yet realised so much as we paid for it).

Having sent this despatch, Sir Charles Wood waited confidently for Lord Stanley's expected question, and when it came, soon after the opening of the session, on March 13th, 1860, he promised unconditionally to the House the restoration of Dhar to its young prince when he came of age, and persuaded the House, by the use of ambiguous language, that the only penalty inflicted on Dhar, would be, at a time when all India was being taxed heavily to pay the expense of the war, the confiscation of an outlying district worth between £2,000 and £3,000 a year.

And so once more the affair seemed happily settled. Nobody here knew the real value of Bhairseah; in the enthusiasm of the moment the prize-money was forgotten, and Sir Charles Wood's public assurances were so cordially repeated in private, that all suspicion was laid asleep, and when the Blue-book was presented to Parliament next year, nobody in this busy London world then cared to read papers, whose interest, it was supposed, had entirely passed away.

There was one, however, who evidently had a misgiving from the first, viz., the late Sir Richmond Shakespeare, who had then succeeded Sir Robert Hamilton as agent to Governor-General for Central India. He had noted the condition attached to the restoration of the Government to the young Rajah, " if he should then be reported qualified to undertake " it ; " and finding that Government had sanctioned the appointment of a British officer, on a salary of £1,200 a year,* to manage the State till the Rajah was " reported qualified," Sir Richmond determined to have a man whom he could trust to do the business, and teach the young Rajah how to do it, so he asked for Captain Wood from Hosunghabad, declaring that: " Everything will depend upon the qualifications of the " officer. He will have a delicate and difficult duty to " perform."† Such an application could not be refused; Captain Wood was appointed, and well he did his work during the six months he remained at Dhar; initiating the young Rajah into more details of administration during that time, than he has been allowed to learn in the next three years.

And Sir Richmond Shakespeare did more than this. On the plea that the former orders of Government

---

* It is believed by the natives that this piece of patronage, which is a convenient stepping-stone for youngsters with good interest, is the greatest obstacle to justice in the case.

† Parliamentary Paper, No. 30, of 1861, page 72, para. 31.

about Dhar had been announced by Proclamation, he issued a Proclamation, without reference to Government, announcing that the young Rajah's possessions " were " restored to him from that time," and promising, absolutely and without any conditions, that " the manage- " ment of them should be made over to him on his " attaining his majority."*

This Proclamation was a complete poser for the Government at the time. They could not recall it without unmasking a fraudulent intention, and yet such words bound them very awkwardly, both to the Rajah and the public. At first they did not know what to do. On the 13th of June, 1860, Lord Canning merely noticed the irregularity of the proceeding. On the 19th of December, Sir Charles Wood not merely noticed the irregularity, but *restated the condition* of making over the management to the Rajah: "If he " should be qualified to undertake it."†

Accordingly, from the time that the affair was forgotten in England, good care was taken that the Rajah never should be " reported qualified to undertake it." Captain Wood was removed in due course, and then followed four or five youngsters, too fond of field sports, &c., to spare many hours for public business, and too ignorant themselves to teach anyone else their "delicate " and difficult duties;" while the minister was appointed with equal forethought, not in one sense without consulting the Rajah's choice, for the person selected had so notoriously a previous misunderstanding with the Rajah, that friendly communication between them on business matters was impossible; and so it is easy to

* Parliamentary Paper, No. 30, of 1861, pages 76, 77.
† Parliamentary Paper, No. 30, of 1861, pages 77, 78.

keep up the farce of periodically reporting the Rajah, "not qualified to undertake the Government."

Now I assert, on the contrary, that he is perfectly qualified to do so. He is a gentle and amiable young man, master of three languages, of more than average intelligence, and frank enough with his friends, though he is naturally reserved with those whom he has every reason to fear and distrust. In fact the pretence of his incompetency is the most transparent hypocrisy. The law has decided, in every civilised country, after far more experience, and with far higher authority than can belong to any individual judgment, the age at which every man in the full possession of his faculties should attain his majority, and be qualified to administer his estate, whether public or private. The law did decide this epoch in the life of the young Rajah of Dhar, at the date of the 8th of April, 1862, when the prince attained 18 years of age, which corresponds to an age of two or three years later among the inhabitants of a colder climate; and the law had decided so justly in the present instance, that not only the Rajah's own subjects, but his neighbours far and near in the province of Malwa, felt there could be no doubt of his competency to govern, and entertained the most sanguine hopes that the repeated public promises of the Government, both in England and India, would be fulfilled by our handing over the power we held in trust for him. They felt that this case would be the test of our professions of renouncing the policy of "annexation;" and they now feel that if the local Government is permitted by the Queen and Parliament of England to break its positive and publicly proclaimed promises; to violate their law; to treat with contempt their opinion; and to virtually annex Dhar, by an indefinite charge of incompetency against its prince; that similar pretexts will never be wanting in the minority of Native princes; that the promised right of adoption will be a mockery; and that no Native State will be safe in future from the grasping foreigners, who have resumed their work by breaking their reiterated pledges to restore the principality of Dhar.

CHAPTER VII.

CONCLUSION.—*Two distinct policies are in presence on this occasion—Old political parties are resisting a new policy.*

Now if the reader will take a brief retrospect of the leading facts of this case, I think he may be inclined to ask whether some further explanation is not still required; and whether the effects produced, considered as a whole, do not indicate the existence of some deeper cause for the fluctuation of our policy towards Dhar, than any I have yet mentioned?

Let it be remembered that, in spite of the orders of a Secretary of State for India, Lord Stanley, backed by a strong current of public opinion at home, in spite of repeated notices of the subject in the House of Commons, in spite of the utmost opposition of the Agent to Governor-General for Central India, Sir R. Hamilton, and his demonstration of the innocence of the Native Government, the following penalties have already been inflicted on Dhar:—

1st. The Rajah was formally deposed six years ago, and has not yet had the management of his State restored to him.

2nd. Not merely the State income, but the revenues appropriated to the support of the Rajah's family and ministers were seized in 1858, and the whole interval between the confiscation of the State and the compulsory partial restitution in 1860, was employed in trying to intimidate and starve the Ranee and her faithful adherents into submitting quietly to the loss of their Raj, so that when at last orders were passed by the Government of India to make an allowance to the Ranee, the news only reached the unfortunate lady a few days before her death, on August 10th, 1860, when she literally sunk, at thirty-two years of age, under the humiliations, the want, the fears, and anguish she had been suffering for the last two years.

3rd. On the second promise to restore the Raj, one-fifth of its income was taken away by the confiscation of Bhairseah.

4th. The treasure and jewels of the State, valued at £80,000, were seized, the heirlooms of the family were sold by public auction (to the inexpressible disgust of the people), and the proceeds were divided as prize-money, of which it was stated last year that every private soldier would receive about £40.*

Is it not plain to any political head that these things could not have been done, and done with perfect impunity, without the support of a powerful party in this country? This is the point we must come to at last. There are no Directors now to be the "buffers" of the State carriage. It is no longer time to stop at this or that "official trained up under the annexation

---

* See "Homeward Mail," Sept. 14th, 1863, page 767.

"system." The executive officers are but subordinates after all: who has been behind them, who instructed them, and to whom did they look for support?

This is a grave question, which I mean to answer as clearly as I have raised it. There has been too long a popular fallacy that the "annexation system" was a pure invention of Lord Dalhousie Probably no experienced man ever believed that a young Colonial Governor, as Lord Dalhousie was then, would venture, without authority, to announce the fundamental change of policy proclaimed in his Sattara Minute, or would have been permitted to carry it into execution in the sweeping style he did, throughout his administration, without the deliberate sanction and previous consent of the Home Government. Yet the public have been credulous enough to believe that he did so, although it is as contrary to the invariable practice of Government to permit any officer they employ to reverse an established system, without asking their leave, on any vital question of State policy, as it is contrary to the practice of public servants to commit such an intolerable act of insubordination. For it is well explained by Mr. Ludlow, who sums up all previous arguments on the subject, that the "annexation system" was the direct reversal of our former policy of non-annexation; which had been approved till then, by almost every great Anglo-Indian statesman or writer, of whom he enumerates some fifteen or sixteen, from the Duke of Wellington down to Colonel Alves.

Moreover, independent of the well-known principles of Government, which forbid us to believe that Lord Dalhousie could have ventured to initiate such an important policy as the "annexation system," without the sanction of the Home Government, I will mention another reason for disbelieving it, besides this induction from the rules and habits of official life. A gentleman who has held some of the highest official appointments in India, and whose honored name is one of those best known to Anglo-Indians, told me that a friend of his was staying at Bowood, the late Lord Lansdowne's country-seat, when the question of "annexation" was discussed by a meeting of the leaders of the Whig party,* and decided in the affirmative, *before ever Lord Dalhousie went to India;* and that many of the claptrap arguments in its favour, which we have been used to read in his Minutes, or in the pages of Mr. George Campbell, date from that meeting at Bowood,† when Lord Dalhousie had not yet left this country. If this be true, and I do not doubt its truth, though I cannot give every one the same conviction by mentioning the name of my informant, it certainly makes Lord Dalhousie's apparent rashness disappear, and leaves him only responsible for the manner in which he carried out this policy, and not for its matter. But, as I said before, the fact of the deliberate sanction and previous consent of the Home Government, might have been induced from known principles of Government, by those

---

* At the time when the "15 millions" deficit of the Affghan war was coming home to their business and bosoms.

† In thus tracing back to the old Whigs, the "grasping" policy which provoked a rebellion, it is but fair to add that I do not suspect the existence of any sympathy for that policy in the breasts of younger members of the present Cabinet; such as Mr. Gladstone, Mr. Cardwell, Mr. Villiers, Mr. Milner Gibson, Lord de Grey and Ripon, &c.

who never heard the above anecdote; and if once it is understood that the Whigs were committed, as a party, to the policy so boldly proclaimed and acted on by Lord Dalhousie, this connection between a great English party and the annexation system, will explain, not only the injustice done to Dhar, as well as many other States, and the projects of farther annexation now hatching in India, but all the resistance offered to Lord Stanley's views, from first to last.

It was then distinctly a "new policy" that was announced by Lord Stanley's advice, in the Queen's Proclamation of 1858, and was simultaneously acted upon, by revoking the confiscation of all the landed estates in Oude, by "disallowing the policy of annexa-" tion" in the case of Dhar, by measures to stop the scandalous Enam resumptions, &c.

It was a new policy of the Derby Cabinet, diametrically opposed to that of their predecessors, the Whigs, and which has not been fairly carried out, owing to the opposition of the Whigs.

That Proclamation contained, among others, the following gracious promise to the Princes of India:—
" We desire no extension of our present territorial pos-
" sessions, and, while we will permit no aggression upon
" our dominions, or our rights, to be attempted with
" impunity, we shall sanction no encroachment on
" those of others. We shall respect the rights, dignity,
" and honor of Native Princes as our own." This promise, then, although merely the revival of our former Conservative system in India, was clearly " a " new policy" in 1858; so that Mr. Ludlow divined the true importance of the Proclamation, when he

named it, with curious felicity, "British India's Magna "Charta,"* and prophesied that, in spite of the evil influences that would be at work from the first to strangle its pledges, the Proclamation would survive every violation of its promises, and would settle the principles of our future Anglo-Indian rule. Some of his phrases cast a rainbow of hope over the dark clouds of opposition he foresaw; for instance, " Words " of grace and justice, once put forth, have a power, as " it were, to draw up men's acts towards their own " level." Again, " How often was Magna Charta " broken, how often confirmed, before it came to be " what it is now, the very corner-stone of our social " state?"

I believe that Mr. Ludlow's anticipations will be eventually realised, and that the "new policy" promised by the Proclamation of 1858, and so cordially welcomed at the time, by England as well as India,† must be carried into effect, sooner or later, by the impulse of public opinion. But the performance of its promises has been delayed, and is still stubbornly resisted by the old evil influences; and, in the case of Dhar, it is plain that nothing but the expression of

---

* " Thoughts on the Policy of the Crown towards India," page 7.

† I mean the "people of India "—of course I do not forget the hostile spirit in which this conciliatory proclamation was received by " the Services," and the contrast between their passive, and not always passive, resistance to the " new policy," and its enthusiastic welcome by the natives (*Vide* Mr. Ludlow's book, just cited, pages 9, 10, and 364 to 367). But the Services will not permanently oppose the will of the nation: if they see that their country is determined to act, in India, on the just and conciliatory principles proclaimed by Lord Stanley, they are patriotic enough to adopt them, whether they like them at first or not.

public opinion can force an old Whig Minister, with whom annexation is a confirmed habit, " to respect the " rights, dignity, and honor of a Native Prince." I have done all I can do by giving a statement of the facts; and I trust that members of Parliament who have been duped, like myself, by the unconditional promises of the Indian Minister, in public and private, will summon him to keep his word, to abolish the miserable piece of patronage that stands in the way of justice, and to hand over the management of his possessions to the much-wronged Rajah of Dhar.

APPENDICES.

APPENDIX A.

Lord Ellenborough's Evidence before Select Committee on Indian Territories, June 18th, 1852.—Question 2,305.

"I consider that in fact our Government is at the head of a system composed of Native States, and I would avoid taking what are called 'rightful occasions of appropriating' the territories of Native States; on the contrary, I should be disposed, as far as I could, to maintain the Native States, and I am satisfied that the maintenance of the Native States, and the giving to the subjects of those States the conviction that they were considered permanent parts of the general Government of India, would materially strengthen our authority. It was impossible for me not to see the respect which our own soldiers entertained for Native Princes. I felt satisfied that I never stood so strong with my own army as when I was surrounded by Native Princes; they like to see respect shown to their Native Princes. I observed, on all occasions, that at the commencement of any interview between the Governor-General and a Native Prince, there was a coldness, and suspicion, and jealousy, and after the Governor-General had treated the Native Prince upon the footing of equality, and received him with honour, the whole feeling of the Native Prince, of all his court, of all his people, and of all his soldiers, was entirely changed: and when I paid the return visit to that Prince, I saw that I had the confidence of the people and of his court and army; it was the consideration shown to their chief that created that great change in their feelings. The Native Princes are sovereigns of one-third of the population of Hindostan; and with reference to the future condition of the country, it becomes more and more important to give them confidence, that no systematic attempt will be made to take advantage of the failure of heirs to confiscate their property, or to injure, in any respect, those sovereigns in the position they at present occupy."

APPENDIX B.

Extract from " India under a Bureaucracy," by J. Dickinson, published in 1853, pages 164, 165.

"They do not take these things so quietly in the country as we do here. We hear of the absorption of a Native State, and go about our business, and think no more of the matter; like a ship's crew, who duly note in the log, 'run down a vessel in the night, all hands lost;' then pursue their voyage and forget it. But these things lodge and rankle in men's minds in India, where too many of our troops are interested in this question of adoption; and, as I said before, the free press is doing its work.

" I am convinced that the Government will, some day, regret the system that is making so many enemies. It will, some day, absorb a Native State too many, and feel a pang like one who has put a fruit into his mouth with a hornet in it. We must not expect the Rajput princes to lie still like oysters, waiting to be dredged. They are, and ever were, a high-spirited, martial race, prompt to appeal to the sword, and just the men to say in a fit of exasperation, ' better an end with fear, than fear without an end.' Meanwhile, the Natives have a stereotyped expression for us, which gives us a false confidence. We tread on ice, and forget the current of passion flowing beneath, which imperils our footing. The Natives seem what they know we expect them to appear, and we do not see their real feelings; we know not how hot the stove may be under its polished surface. For the fire is not out; we are obliged to keep it up by our Native army, which may blaze into a conflagration, and burn the empire. There may be some Procida, matchless in diplomatic art and tenacity of purpose, who will travel for years to knit enemies against us; who will mine the ground under our feet, and lay the train of combustibles; there may be some outrage, which will suddenly raise a cry, terrible as that which broke forth when the bells of Monreale were sounding to vespers, a cry of ' death to the Englishmen;' there may be some conspiracy of which, as at Vellore, we have not even a suspicion, until the Native regiments open their fire on our barracks; and, as a merchant who is obliged to throw all his treasure overboard to save the ship, a storm may arise in India which will cost us more to maintain our power than all we have gained, or can ever hope to gain, by our confiscations."

APPENDIX C.

Fallacy that the Punjab saved India.

The officials who were responsible for this enormous blunder of leaving Bengal, the seat of our Empire, with its forts, arsenals, stores, treasure, and communications, at the mercy of a disaffected Sepoy army, at a time when misgovernment had filled India with causes for insurrection, subsequently invented the phrase, "the Punjab saved India," to conceal their folly. But however the popular belief in this fallacy that "the Punjab saved India" may be kept up for a while by journals in the interest of the government, the truth must come out at last that the Punjab "almost lost India!" by embarrassing its finances, and by *absorbing the European force which would either have prevented or have at once crushed the mutiny.* As for "saving India," if the Governor of the Punjab had not sent back a portion of his European force to the provinces where we were fighting for existence, when he was in no personal danger whatever himself, he would have been a worse traitor than the Sepoys were; but the sending reinforcements to the besiegers of Delhi only began the work of "saving India:" witness the dangers and difficulties encountered by Lord Clyde and Sir Hugh Rose in subsequent campaigns!

A few words will explain the financial effect of annexing the Punjab, and that peculiar good fortune of being exempt from personal danger, which distinguished the Governor of the Punjab from every other Governor in India during the Rebellion.

To begin with the finances: In the year 1857, besides the excess of European strength allotted to the Punjab, it had a Native force of various descriptions, partly Sepoys, and partly their hereditary enemies the Sikhs.* There were 44,000 Sepoys, with some Sikhs among them; 12,000 police, horse and foot, all disciplined soldiers; 10,000 called detective police, and a large body (number unknown) of village watchmen. The total army of the Punjab numbered, with camp-followers, about 400,000 men! and therefore it is not surprising that this province entailed an annual loss on the finances of India of *upwards of two millions sterling*, as Lord Canning proved in his

---

* And I must observe that although the orders of the government were not fully carried out, and very few Sikhs were recruited, it was, in my opinion, a great mistake to introduce any of them into regiments raised from the Natives of Hindoostan. Such a step could not fail to rouse the suspicions of those races who for generations, from father to son, had supplied the men of our Native army: it seemed evident that the government no longer trusted to them, when it was gradually arming and substituting for themselves, their most dangerous enemies.

Minute of November, 1861. With regard to the other point: At the very beginning of the mutiny, the danger in the Punjab disappeared almost within twenty-four hours, owing to the extraordinary energy of Mr., now Sir Robert, Montgomery. On the 11th of May news arrived at Lahore that a Sepoy mutiny had broken out on the previous evening at Meerut. On the following morning, May 12th, a hurried telegram announced the seizure of Delhi, on which Sir Robert Montgomery immediately made up his mind that a crisis of the first magnitude had arrived, and that he would deal with it as such. Accordingly, as Sir John Lawrence was then in the North, at Rawul Pindee, and there was no time for communicating with him (in fact, the destiny of the Punjab was decided before he could get back to Lahore !) Montgomery determined to act at once in the most decisive way, on his own responsibility; so, without interrupting a grand ball and supper which took place the same evening, his preparations were rapidly and quietly made, and at daybreak next morning the Sepoy regiments at Meean Meer were disarmed without a blow; Ferozapore, with its immense magazines, was secured a few hours later, and expresses had been despatched to all the stations previously, announcing the strong measures taken at the capital, and putting all our officers on their guard, which ensured the securing of all the important stations, and the disarming of the Sepoys everywhere during the following month, not always without local risk, but always without the central power of the Punjab Government being ever endangered again for an instant.

Nor was the disarmament of the Sepoys the only source of security to Sir John Lawrence: the spirit of the Sikh people, and of the neighbouring Native Princes, was at least as great an assurance. I have already alluded to the "blood-feud" between the Sikhs and the Hindoostanees, dating from the atrocities perpetrated in the 18th century, by the Mogul Emperors, and not diminished by our conquest of the Punjab with Sepoy armies. Perhaps it may be interesting to give an example of this hereditary hostility, which has never to my knowledge appeared in print. Down to the period of the mutiny there was always a large annual attendance of Sikhs at the great fair and famous shrines of Hurdwar, on the Ganges, and most of them travelled on foot, making long and hurried marches, often of 30 miles a day. Nevertheless it was their habit to stop at Sirhind, and traverse the ruins, which are many miles in extent, and at least a quarter of a mile from the road at their nearest point, thus wasting precious time, and going far out of their way, merely for the pleasure of making a visit to Sirhind, which always ended by their taking up a brick, spitting upon it, and throwing it down, with the vow, *spoken out, whoever might be looking on,* that as they had "looted" and utterly destroyed Sirhind, so they would one day "loot" and utterly destroy Delhi, and raze every house in the city to its foundations. It was clear that such fellows would make pretty warm allies against the Hindoos; and it was not long before they showed what stuff they were made of.

On the 14th of May, the day after the regiments at Meean Meer were disarmed, a report spread that they would make a rush for a neighbouring station, where a Sepoy regiment still retained its arms. The experienced officer in charge of the district, who knew the antipathy that existed between the races, undertook " to raise a human barrier of villagers across their road," and appealed to the country people. The agriculturists of the neighbourhood, who, as it happened, had formed the flower of the Khalsa army, and afterwards furnished us with a splendid corps of artillerymen, veterans from Runjeet Singh's army, these men turned out at once to fight and stop the Sepoys; they barricaded the road, watched a whole night, very nearly came to blows with a detachment of English, whom they took for the Sepoy advance guard, and thus showed from the beginning, as on every subsequent opportunity, that Sikhs were at least as hostile to Sepoys as Englishmen could be, while they were as much more dangerous, in proportion as they were less scrupulous than Englishmen. (A Sepoy always carried his money on his person, and possessed generally £5 at least, in his normal condition, while those who had plundered the treasuries had often £50 a piece: they were too well worth killing to expect any quarter from Sikhs!)

The result of this popular demonstration in the Punjab, within two days after the appearance of the crisis, and of similar ones on the following days, showed that the old feud between the races was as strong as ever, and would give us a most powerful and warlike ally against Hindoostanees in the Sikh population. Consequently, when a Sepoy regiment was disarmed, the Sikh element in its ranks had their arms restored to them; we used the purely Sikh corps freely in disarming the Sepoys; and having the immediate and cordial adherence of the neighbouring Princes, the Rajahs of Cashmere, Puttealah, Bikaneer, Bhawulpore, Kuppoorthullah, &c., to confirm the loyalty of the Punjabees, we began at once to recruit an army of Sikhs to invade and "loot Hindoostan;" while the Sepoys at Delhi were fools enough to whet their appetite for revenge, by mutilating some of their Sikh prisoners in the most cruel way, and sending them back to General Barnard's camp in that state, as an example of the vengeance they meant to take on the whole nation. Finally, it happened that the Sikhs were agitated at that very time by a remarkable prophecy, (which, strange to say, was literally fulfilled!) that they, in conjunction with "Topee Wallahs" ("hat wearers," or the British), who should come over the sea, would reconquer Delhi, and place the head of the King's son on the very spot where the head of Gooroo Teg Bahadoor had been exposed one hundred and eighty years before, by the son of Aurungzebe.* Afterwards, when Hodson captured the old King, and

---

* By the way, it is known that after the murder of his wife and children, Govind Gooroo escaped to the Deccan, but it is not generally known, *except to the Sikhs*, that their saint has a shrine at Hyderabad! a dangerous lure for those reckless, daring fellows, who would go to the ends of the earth for "loot." The best of the Sikhs, Jats, are by nature first-rate agriculturists; and to send our Sikh army back to the plough, would be better for them, and safer for us.

shot his sons, his Sikh ressaldar, remembering the oracle, exposed their bodies for three days on the same spot. These facts show that the Governor of the Punjab was in no personal danger whatever, and he could not have avoided sending reinforcements to Delhi without the most cowardly and criminal neglect of duty.

But certain parties have combined to puff Sir John Lawrence as the "Saviour of the Empire!" and if nobody else has sufficient courage to come forward and do so, I must, if I stand alone, deny his claim to such a title; because it involves the greatest injustice to other men, and especially to the (yet unannexed) Native Princes of India.

For instance, it was stated circumstantially by the *Times* of December 1st, 1863, that "when the existence of our power in India depended on the success of the siege of Delhi,"—"the siege of Delhi owed its success to Sir John Lawrence," and "would have been abandoned without his energetic remonstrances;"—that "with nothing but a small military force, and his own undaunted courage to rely on," in the midst of a hostile population, "only waiting for the least symptom of weakness to rise in insurrection," Sir John Lawrence contrived to suppress the mutiny of his own Native troops, to "hold his province without any of those disastrous reverses which befel us in other parts;" and "out of his own slender resources" to send troops, and stores, and artillery to Delhi, "in a position in which it would have been thought a great triumph for him even to preserve the Punjab." Well, I have already answered some of these assertions with regard to the "hostile population," the "small military force," and the "slender resources;" another of them, that the siege of Delhi would have been abandoned but for Sir John Lawrence's energetic remonstrances, was contradicted in the next day's *Times* by Lord Lyveden; and the remaining assertion, that the siege owed its success to Sir John Lawrence, was thus contradicted by anticipation in "the *Times* of India," of July 9th, 1863: "The charge against Lord Canning was, that he lacked decision and daring, and we hardly know what else of the kindred virtues. But it subsequently transpired, and we suppose it will startle the writer of '*Our Paper*' considerably to be told the fact, that Sir John Lawrence, famous as he is for decision, hesitated and broke down at the siege of Delhi. He advised a treaty with the insurgents, and so did the General in command! We owed it to the vacillating, undecided Canning that the treaty book was not polluted with a compact with the assassins of Meerut and Delhi." I do not quote the above to substitute one hero-worship for another; I object to any of them. In the fearful crisis of 1857, every Englishman did his best, as a matter of course, and it seems invidious to proclaim any one of them, as the *Times*, on such unsubstantial grounds, proclaims Sir John Lawrence, the "Saviour of the Empire!" Moreover, it is unjust to the enlightened portion of the Natives of India, who supported us through the struggle, as I show in the text.

I know it may seem as if I liked to be always in opposition, if I venture just now to differ from the popular estimate of Sir John

Lawrence, when the press, and the political leaders on both sides, have hailed him by acclamation as the best qualified Governor-General, that ever embarked for India. But if I cannot suppress the light that is in me, it is not because I "like to be always in opposition;" on the contrary, after having worked hard so many years for India, and having lived to see every part of the original programme of the India Reform Society admitted to be right in principle, and more or less carried out in practice, I cannot *like to be* for ever in " disgrace " with men in power, honored with no distinction that they can withhold from me, and the object of unconcealed aversion or suspicion to their legion of friends and dependents. Yet I have strong reasons for regarding the appointment of Sir John Lawrence with anxiety and alarm: and not the less so because I admit all that is said of his energy and ability. At a time when I see so many symptoms of a revival of Lord Dalhousie's system in India, in reliance on a British army of 80,000 men, I cannot forget that Sir John Lawrence was the most uncompromising agent of that system. Sir John trusted to force, as instinctively as his brother, Sir Henry Lawrence, trusted to justice and generosity, and in the Punjab he had an overwhelming force, not only of the Native but the European army, to support his measures. But we cannot govern all India in this " zubberdust " style; or, as a native gentleman once happily expressed it: " You cannot *govern* India on those principles with an army of 300,000 Englishmen, though you might reduce it to a desert with 50,000." The case of Bischen Singh may be familar to a few Anglo-Indians, but scarcely any know how numerous such cases were. Yet it was known to the authorities; for when Lord Ellenborough brought forward this case on July 11th, 1856,—which he did in that style which no orator has ever surpassed and few have equalled,—the sting of the Duke of Argyle's reply was contained in the last sentence of his speech, in which he warned the House to beware what they were about, as a favourable decision on this petition might affect 5,000 or 6,000 other such cases.

No doubt there were thousands of such cases. I am informed that the last time Lord Canning visited the Punjab, when he gave back quietly an immense quantity of lands that had been thus taken by Sir John Lawrence, he was so astonished at the numbers of petitioners, and the strength of their claims, that he asked why they had never complained to him before ? The answer was : " If we had complained of John Lawrence, we should have been stripped, not only of all he had taken, but of all he had left us." In fact, the system of ruining the Native aristocracy, and removing everything between our government and the cultivator of the soil, was carried on as vigorously in the Punjab as in any part of India; and therefore I say, God forbid that the new Governor-General should bring back the old " grasping " system !

Another reason for a word of warning. The greatest difficulty India Reformers had to encounter twelve or fourteen years ago was the profound respect paid by everybody in England to the " authority of the Governor-General." For this reason, all the pamphlets, and speeches, and petitions from India in the year 1853 went for nothing. Even the decision of a Cabinet Council on a Saturday, was reversed on the following Monday, in deference to the oracle from India. And this overwhelming " authority " was produced by a combination of parties beyond what even the philosophic Mill could foresee. It was not only the Minister, whose interest it was " to prevent inspection, to lull suspicion asleep, to ward off inquiry, to inspire a blind confidence. to praise incessantly the management of affairs in India, and, by the irresistible force of his influence, make other people praise it; "* it was not only the Minister who " smothered complaint " (and a Minister has always a number of disinterested friends to do his work, in Parliament, in the press, and in private society), but the religious world joined in the concert of praise, because of the Governor-General's zeal for the propagation of Christianity in India. This consideration induced the Christians of Exeter Hall, headed by powerful leaders in and out of Parliament, to swallow everything, before the India Reform Society put them to shame—annexations, resumptions, mal-administration in the judicial system, in the police system, in the system of taxation, of public works, of the employment of Natives in the public service, even of the practice of torture—they digested everything, to unite with the Government in raising the authority of a Governor-General, so zealous for the propagation of Christianity in India. Now, therefore, when I see the same combination of parties employed to raise above all questioning the " authority " of the new Governor-General, remembering the difficulty we had before, I naturally wish to warn the public in time, that the former administration of Sir John Lawrence was not faultless, and that, although I sincerely hope his future course may be so, if he does make any mistakes, it should not again require a rebellion, a dozen years of discussion, and as much evidence and expense as a dozen great trials in courts of law, to make people believe him fallible.

* Mill's Hist. of India, Vol. iv., page 571.

APPENDIX D.

Extracts from Memoir of Sir Claude Wade, in the Annual Report of the Royal Asiatic Society, 1862.

"It may be worth while to state here, in his own words, those simple principles by which Sir Claude Wade achieved such extraordinary success in all his future intercourse with the "Lion of the Punjaub" (Runjeet Singh). 'I used my best endeavours,' he said, ' to follow the example of Lord Metcalfe in balancing the interests of the two States, and identifying their policy, as paramount to every other object. In India, it is essential to the proper care and preservation of our system of alliances, that the British Agent should be regarded as a friend of the chiefs among whom he resides, rather than as a mere instrument for conveying the instructions or enforcing the policy of their foreign masters. Our rigid rule is not congenial with their national habits, and a softening agency may wisely be exercised to inspire the confidence of our Indian allies, without losing sight of the views and interests of our own country.' -. . . . .

"It is worthy of remark that, although dealing throughout the greater part of his career with men of the sword, who appeared to recognise no authority but that of force, Sir Claude Wade never had occasion to employ military means to effect his objects during the whole course of his agencies at Loodiana or Indore."

APPENDIX E.

(*From the Times of India, July* 28, 1861).

" The appointment of Colonel Durand to the Foreign Secretaryship at Calcutta, in the room of Mr. Barnes, is, we learn from the Home Secretary's speech in Parliament on the 6th ultimo, desiderated by no less a personage than the Viceroy himself.

" ' Lord Canning had written home, proposing that a member of the Indian Council, Colonel Durand, should go out to India, and take the place of Foreign Secretary; that gallant officer being most eminently fitted, in the opinion of the Governor-General, for the office.' Colonel Durand has responded to the invitation, and the whole ' of the Indian Council were perfectly willing that the Government of India should have the assistance desired. Yet, under the existing law, the appointment could not be made.'

" We are prepared to accord so much praise to Colonel Durand's personal and professional character, that some of our readers may possibly think us guilty of inconsistency, in suggesting, after all, that such an appointment is by no means desirable. But it is the fact that Colonel Durand's failure as a Political has been as conspicuous as his merits as a soldier. Sir Charles Wood could hardly have chosen a more unhappy illustration of the necessity of throwing open the Civil Service to outsiders, than the desire to appoint Colonel Durand to an office for which he is eminently unfit. That Colonel Durand possesses great talents and ability of a high order, with indefatigable perseverance, we admit cheerfully, but his antecedents show that he is not the man to be used with advantage in political employ. As an engineer, we believe, Colonel Durand stands in the foremost ranks of the army; and no man probably has a better knowledge of, or more complete insight into, our whole military system than he, while the services rendered by him in the field in the Affghan War were conspicuous and real.

" Had Lord Canning, therefore, desired Colonel Durand's presence in Calcutta as Military Secretary, or Military Member of Council, we should have hailed the appointment possibly with delight, certainly with satisfaction. But as Foreign Secretary we apprehend it were impossible for a more unpopular nomination to have been made, short of Colonel Ramsay, of Nepaul. It is becoming of increasing importance, day by day, that our political agents all over India should be distinguished by their mastery of the accomplishments, or possession of the natural grace, by which intercourse with the Native princes of the country are so materially assisted, while the want of that grace or of those accomplishments has been conspicuous throughout the whole of Colonel Durand's political career. The whole responsibility of the selection rests, it seems, upon Lord Canning, and we are certainly curious to know what infatuation can have suggested this extraordinary nomination. Colonel Durand's administration whilst at Moulmein will hardly, we presume, be allowed to be the ground of his selection, any more than his success at Gwalior during the few short months of his office there, which led to the expulsion of the Tarabhaee, and the discord and heartburnings that prevailed at the court. At Bhopal, again, do we not find Colonel Durand's evil genius pursuing him still, and leading him to countenance, as pretender to the Musnud, the man who subsequently raised the standard of revolt against us at Indore, and drove Colonel Durand himself out of Malwa? And lastly, at Indore itself, in the terrible crisis of the mutiny, is not the memory of Colonel Durand's failure present to all minds? A failure, too, occurring at one of those moments upon which history waits with 'bated breath.' Distinguished for a cold severity of manner, imperfectly acquainted with the vernacular languages, possessing little insight into the character of the people, and strongly prejudiced against them by a constitutional and invincible repugnance, Colonel Durand is perhaps the very last officer whom Lord Canning could advantageously select as the mouth-piece of the Governor-General in public or private Durbar, or as the medium of official communication with the Native courts of the country. As every well-informed man in India knows, it is essential to the success of a political agent that he should be distinguished for imperturbable mildness of manner, dignity of deportment, and perfect command of Court language, while no officer can be aught but a failure who has not learned to sympathise with and feel kindly towards the people in spite of the peculiarities which we admit and deplore. Colonel Durand is constitutionally unfitted for political employ, and the elevation of this gentleman to the head of the political service is one of those strange caprices of patronage which, were it associated with any other name than that of Lord Canning (for whom we have a sincere respect), we should unhesitatingly ascribe to jobbery. At all events, Sir Charles Wood could hardly have stumbled upon a more unhappy illustration of the fact that the public interests required the throwing open of the Civil Service to such officers."

APPENDIX F.

Communications from the Dhar Government which preceded the advance of the British Column.

" Abstract translation of an Urzee from the Dhar Vakeel, 11th October, 1857.

" About 10, P.M., on the 9th instant (Friday), all the Wulaitees in the service of my master, that were on duty at different places in the town, got under arms, and about 100 of them went towards Bhopawur; but it is not exactly known to what place they intended to go. The Mekranees seem also inclined to mutiny. The report of the Agent going to Dhar might have caused this movement.

" Verbal Message.

" Yesterday, 10th, about 9, A.M., all the Mussulmans in the town of Dhar, with a portion of the Sibundee, collecting outside the town, set up a Mahomedan standard. Some Pathans from Mundisore coming in have offered high pays, fifteen and twenty rupees per head. The Budmashes that had gone towards Bhopawur plundered Government mails.

" (True translation).
(Signed) " W. R. SHAKESPEAR,
" *Officiating First Assistant Agent to the Governor-General for Central India.*"*

" To Capt. A. R. E. HUTCHINSON,
" Bheel Agent and Political Assistant, Bhopawur.
" Honored Sir,

" News came just now from Dhar that the Budmash Pathans of that place, accompanied by those of Amjheera, went to Bhopawur, burnt the bungalows, and, taking possession of guns and ammunition, went towards Sirdapore. The bungalows of this place also they burnt, and the guns and ammunition were taken possession of. In the affray which ensued there a Native clerk was wounded by a bullet, and two men killed—the names of whom are not yet discovered. Some men are also killed at Sirdapore, but it is not known who they are. The Budmashes are increasing day by day; therefore you will be kind enough in making arrangements for their punishment, and restoring

---

* Parl. Paper, No. 200, of 1859, page 13.

the tranquility of the State, as it looks to you for assistance. I beg to request that you will not leave the Budmashes unpunished for crimes they had committed.

"In short, the welfare of the State depends on your generosity,
(Signed) "RAGHONATH NARAIN,
Vakeel of Dhar.
"12th October, 1857."

"To Capt. A. R. E. HUTCHINSON,
"Political Assistant and Bheel Agent.

"Honored Sir,

"I received a letter from the Durbar yesterday, dated 11th inst., that the Pathans, with Jamadar Goolkhan and others, went to Bhopawur on the 9th inst., on their way they looted the Dawk. The letter states that several parties of Pathans poured down from all directions at once, and from this the Durbar concludes that there was a mutual settlement amongst them. They fought with the Bheel Corps, wrested from them the guns and ammunition, and set fire to the Bungalow there. This is nothing but oppression and tyranny. It is reported that the Budmashes will return and stop outside the town near the fort. These Budmashes deserve immediate punishment; but the other Sepoys have also an internal communication with them. I hear that these Budmashes have kept picquets on the public road, to prevent communication that way, which is a great obstacle for post to come and go. The Durbar looks to you as its well wisher and supporter, and hopes that you will render any assistance in your power at this critical time. You will not fail to show that kindness at this time which you showed heretofore. It is rumoured that the Budmashes are 1,500 in number.
(Signed) "RAGHONATH NARAIN,
"*Vakeel of Dhar.*

"12th October, 1857."

"Translation of an urzee from the Vakeel of Dhar to the Officiating Agent Governor General for Central India, dated 12th October, 1857, received on the 13th October.

"The Vilaitees and Pathan mercenaries of Dhar mutinying went to Bhopawur, and fighting with the detachment of Malwah Bheel Corps there, and seizing their guns and ammunition, have returned to Dhar, and are encamped outside. What they intend to do next is unknown. No confidence whatever can now be placed in any troops (Seebundees, &c.) so as to employ them against the rebels. Such I have been informed by the Sirkar, and report to you accordingly. The only confidence of the Rajah now is in you, and you should make the best (bundobust) arrangement in your judgment.

"(True translation.)
(Signed) "F. J. H. HELBERT,
"*Assistant Agent Governor General for Central India.*"

APPENDIX G.

Order from Capt. Hutchinson respecting supply of ammunition to rebels.

"Abstract translation of a khareeta from Capt. Hutchinson to the Rajah of Dhar, dated Oct. 23rd, 1857.

"(After compliments). The Durbar professes to be in friendly relations with the British Government, and, on account of this, the Officiating Agent to Governor-General (Col. Durand) has come with a column to assist them. But we hear that the rebels are asking the Durbar to supply them with ammunition (powder and balls), and if the Durbar do so, they will be treated like rebels."

www.ingramcontent.com/pod-product-compliance
Lightning Source LLC
Chambersburg PA
CBHW030403170426
43202CB00010B/1464